THE PIVOT OF

CIVILIZATION

And

A Plan for Peace

By Margaret Sanger

1922

With foreword by Anthony Horvath

Suzeteo Enterprises
συζητεο πραγματων

The Pivot of Civilization

And a Plan for Peace

By Margaret Sanger

With Foreword by Anthony Horvath

Read this book online at www.apologeticslibrary.com

Published by Suzeteo Enterprises. www.suzeteo.com

This edition includes an index to aid the serious student.

ISBN: 978-1-936830-04-6

Contents

The *Real* Pivot of Civilization
By Anthony Horvath

I

Let's play a matching game. Which Nazis wrote the following?

"As Western society comes to distinguish between those forms of euthanasia that are pernicious and those that are therapeutic- an inevitable consequence of our progress toward liberal humanism- expanded access to neonatal euthanasia appears likely."

"The Remedy- If such people were lower animals we would probably kill them off to prevent them from spreading. Humanity won't allow this, but we do have the remedy of separating the sexes in asylums or other places and in various ways preventing intermarriage and the possibilities of perpetuating such a low and degenerate race. Remedies of this sort have been tried successfully in Europe and are now meeting with success in this country."

"Indeed, it has been concluded that compulsory population-control laws, even including laws requiring compulsory abortion, could be sustained under the existing Constitution if the population crisis became sufficiently severe to endanger the society. Few today consider the situation in the United States serious enough to justify compulsion, however."

The emergency problem of segregation and sterilization must be faced immediately. Every feeble-minded girl or woman of the hereditary type, especially of the moron class, should be segregated during the reproductive period. Otherwise, she is almost certain to bear imbecile children, who in turn are just as certain to breed other defectives. .... Moreover when we realize that each feeble-minded person is a potential source of an endless progeny of defect, we prefer the policy of immediate sterilization, of making sure that parenthood is absolutely prohibited to the feeble-minded."

But you can start immediately to eliminate the barely educated, unhealthy and poor segment of our country. No, I'm not advocating some sort of mass extinction of these unfortunate people. Crime, drugs and disease are already doing that. The problem is that their numbers are not only replaced but increased by the birth of millions of babies to people who can't afford to have babies. ... No, government is also going to have to provide vasectomies, tubal ligations and abortions... Even if we make birth control as ubiquitous as sneakers and junk food, there will still be unplanned pregnancies."

So, which Nazi uttered such remarks? Was it Himmler? Josef Mengele? Hitler himself? In actual fact, these are not the words of the Nazis. They are not from Europeans at all, but Americans. The first quote comes from a bioethicist of our own time, Jacob Appel, who essentially argued in a published article that doctors should be able to kill born children who are not expected to have a 'good life.'

And this apart from, and in spite of, parental consent.

The second quote comes from a science text book. That's right, a science text book. And not just any text book, but the one at the heart of the 'Scope's Monkey Trial.' The book was called *Civic Biology* and was written by a man named George William Hunter in the 1920s. We are inclined to think of that trial as a battle between science and religion, evolution against creationism. However, I bet most modern readers have no idea that at this time in American history, the terms 'science' and 'evolution', were intricately bound up with Malthusianism and eugenics. I wager that even staunch evolutionists today would object to Hunter's application of evolutionary principles!

The third quote is found in yet another text book. This one was composed in the 1970s, long after the horrors of the Holocaust dampened the public support for sterilization programs. Moreover, one of the co-authors of that text book is a man named John Holdren. This name may be unfamiliar to the reader. Who is he? Well, as of this writing he is the chief scientist in the Obama administration. Does he still believe, as it appears he once did, that compulsory abortion can be carried out under the U.S. Constitution? His 'assurances,' such as they are, haven't been re-assuring.

The fourth quote is found in the book you are now reading by Margaret Sanger on page 38. Like the *Civic Biology* textbook, Sanger wrote her book in the 1920s, before Hitler had attempted to apply eugenics techniques to Jews, gypsies, blacks, disabled people, and others. In fact, it may even be that Hitler got his idea for concentration camps from Sanger or other 'birth control' proponents. In *A Plan for Peace* (page ix), she writes:

> The first step would thus be to control the intake and output of morons, mental defectives, epileptics.
>
> The second step would be to take an inventory of the secondary group such as illiterates, paupers, unemployables, criminals, prostitutes, dope-fiends; classify them in special departments under government medical protection, and segregate them on farms and open spaces as long as necessary for the strengthening and development of moral conduct.
>
> Having corralled this enormous part of our population and placed it on a basis of health instead of punishment, it is safe to say that fifteen or twenty millions of our population would then be organized into soldiers of defense—defending the unborn against their own disabilities.

The fifth quote springs ahead a few more years. It comes from a letter that a certain Ron Weddington wrote to Bill Clinton, then newly elected to his first term in the presidency. Mr. Weddington, if you didn't know, was co-counsel on the famous Roe vs. Wade Supreme Court case that ruled abortion on demand as constitutional.

Thus, our quotes cover a span of about 90 years and are all from Americans reflecting basically the same kind of thinking, both before and after the Holocaust. Of course, though the Sanger book that you have in your hands today was written in the 1920s, she would later found Planned Parenthood, an organization that persists to this day. Given her guiding principles, stated plainly in this text and others, it is an open question how much her 'pro-choice' organization was really about giving women the 'choice' about what to do with 'their own bodies.' Perhaps she really had in view "morons, mental defectives, epileptics." Perhaps this organization *still* shares this view.

Our quotes don't come from common men off the street who have no power or ability to carry out their stated principles, or influence others to do so. Moreover, they are not the only people who think this way. Not quoted was Peter Singer (but he certainly could have been!), as he urged the human race to sterilize itself and has argued that even a two year old can be killed without raising ethical dilemmas (since it isn't a *person*). Like Jacob Appel, he is a well published academic, transmitting his ideas to the next generation. John Holdren, as already mentioned, is a prominent member of the Obama administration, uniquely placed to influence and carry out policy. On that note, it is worth pointing out that two of our quotes come from text books- the ultimate example of a deliberate attempt to transmit values to the next generation.

All this has been said in order to keep this book, *The Pivot of Civilization*, in proper perspective. It would be nice if we could write it off as an ideological artifact of a past, now rejected, era. Nice, but impossible. As illustrated above, many of the same principles detailed by Sanger are held by academics and policy makers and politicians alive today. This should be cause for concern.

Of course, with the Holocaust in the rear view mirror, even proponents of eugenics, euthanasia, population control, etc, are wary about how their proposals will be construed. No one wants to repeat the mistakes of the past. It begs the question though: given another go at Malthusian population control measures, can we really be confident that this time the social engineers will get it right? And what about the next generation that is receiving these values in their education? How do we know that the next generation will agree that what we call mistakes were mistakes at all?

This type of argument is often waved aside as mere hysterics. Someone may declare the argument defeated according to "Godwin's Law," a whimsical observation that any argument will eventually lead to one of the parties involved comparing the other's viewpoints against Nazi ideology. A variation of the 'Law' is the belief that whoever invokes the Holocaust first in an argument, loses. However, the framer of the 'law' never intended it to be applied to *valid* comparisons to the Holocaust. As illustrated by the quotes above, *these* comparisons are more than valid: the ideas and sentiments expressed *are the same*.

Certainly the quote from Civic Biology about 'success in Europe' and Sanger's call to segregate undesirables "on farms and open spaces" are explicit references to European racial policies and the Nazi concentration camps, no?

"Godwin's Law" was really about the uncanny way that arguments eventually wind their way back to comparing and contrasting ideas against what happened in the Holocaust. I would extend this, arguing that comparisons with 20th century communist purges and the like are also inevitable. Like Godwin, though, I would resist the notion that once this point has been reached the argument can be waved away or dismissed. The comparisons certainly may be valid, and if so, given the proper weight in evaluating the idea in question.

Yet it is more than that. *Why* do arguments eventually, inevitably, turn towards comparisons to the murderous events of the 20th century?

Margaret Sanger believed that the pivot of civilization would turn on how civilization managed its own evolution. She was not alone. Tens of thousands of people rose to the challenge. They had the courage of their convictions. They had the assurance that science was on their side. (See Chapter X of this book!) They were convinced that they possessed at last the definitive explanation of reality, buttressed by the arguments of Malthus and the evidence of Darwin, and that this explanation carried with it certain, inevitable, logical consequences. *Res ipsa loquitur.*

The *actual* consequence of their beliefs applied was hell on earth.

In the 20th century, millions upon millions of people died in camps, gulags, secluded fields, and private chambers. The Nazis and the communists were enemies but they shared the view that it was time for brave and scientific people to chart their own evolutionary course. The final death toll of their work, factoring in deaths from famine or other incidental casualties, probably tops some 500,000,000 individuals... dead. This is apart from the question of the tremendous loss of liberty and wealth that affected as many more.

With such events in our relatively recent past is only makes sense that all ideas would eventually be compared against the ideas that led to such atrocities. The bloodshed of the 20th century turns out to be the locus of the *real* pivot of civilization. Sanger thought that population control would be the pivot of civilization. It now appears that the consequences of that thinking is the true pivot. Against those consequences, all things are now compared.

III

Ideas can be very dangerous things but they are never so dangerous as when they find themselves rooted in someone brave enough to actually carry them out. Thus, it is important that we carefully consider what we believe and why, being careful to test our ideas against our moral code. If in this test we find that the ideas war against our morality, we have two choices: reject the ideas emphatically, or be brave enough to adjust our moral code.* Moreover, we must consider not only whether or not our moral code might allow for the atrocities that occurred in the 20th century, but also whether or not it might, if logically followed, actually require repeating those atrocities. Many people are sickened by the bloody history of the last century but they actually have a similar moral code as those who brought it about.

Reading Sanger's book can be a useful service, prompting the reader to seriously consider their beliefs and the foundations for their beliefs. Coming as it does before the great calamities, it is unashamed of connecting dots in explicit terms. It is bold in a way that is startling and shocking to the reader who is unaware that Sanger's arguments were actually common fare during the era. And they were very common indeed.

Unfortunately, they are still common today.

Are they yours?

The question is worth asking and if you are an honest and brave person, you will ask it. Do you accept as fact the evolutionary account that Sanger and her ilk believe 'spoke for itself'? Isn't it obvious that if religion is fraudulent and we are evolved that the good and proper thing to do is to take charge of our evolution? You don't think so? What are your reasons? Do you have any? Rejecting this conclusion, taken as self-evident by virtually all of those who first faced the evidence, merely because you recoil in horror at how they acted on the evidence is not an argument: it is cowardice.

At least, that is what would have been thought by Sanger and others before history unfolded before them. Some still think it is cowardice today.

But there is another option. You may not be a coward, after all. It may rather be that there is something inside you that cries out in pain and despair at the bloody injustice of it all. There is something inside of you that says: "These may indeed be the logical implications of these facts, but my humanity will not tolerate it!"

For those who have not had their humanity yet driven out of them, this indeed is often precisely what is going on. Surely, though, you see the

---

* See, for example, page 10 of this book.

contradiction: The 'facts' are that humans are mere beasts... there is no soul, they have no intrinsic value... they obey the same principles of natural selection: only the fittest survive... there is nothing special about humans. In spite of these facts, you know that humans are more. Much more. They are special. They are not to be treated like beasts. They are not to be burned alive in ovens or gassed or segregated into camps to make sure they don't reproduce without permission from the government. They are not to be rounded up in purges and shot because they do not subscribe to Marxist ideology with 100% orthodoxy.

Where did you get *this* belief?

As it happens, I spoke to soon. The 'pivot of civilization' isn't even the macabre events of the 20th century. It must have something to do with how we perceive reality itself in general and how we perceive the nature of humans in particular. There is a thread woven all the way through this conversation that has not yet been tugged at and brought to attention for inspection. That thread is the implicit purpose of everyone involved- the eugenicists, Sanger, Holdren, Appel, you, the reader, and me, the author- to seek out and do the *good* thing and avoid the *bad* thing.

Here we come face to face with *the* problem: on the 'scientific' evolutionary view, things like 'good' and 'bad' are completely relative and subjective terms. The only way in which these can be grounded in objective reality is if we frame them in evolutionary principles such as 'survival of the fittest.' 'Good' will be that which helps us to survive to reproduce and perform better in the competition for scarce resources. 'Bad' will be that which doesn't. Yet, when we saw a generation actually brave enough to act on this, unspeakable calamities followed. Whatever this might say about the veracity of the evolutionary account, it says at minimum that it cannot be the final word about 'goodness' and 'badness.' The turning in our stomach when we see corpses stacked up like cordwood is enough to demonstrate this.

The real pivot of civilization will have to center somehow in the value we place on human life. If this is subjective, death at the hands of other humans is inevitable. If it is objective, we will die to prevent that very thing. But how could it ever be objective?

A thing only has value when something 'higher' than it imparts it. A dollar has no value intrinsic to itself. It is just a piece of paper with ink and scribbles on it. It only has value insofar as humans regard it with value amongst themselves. A dollar interacting with other dollars is perfectly allowed to treat other dollars as they know themselves to really be: pulped wood and cloth with chemicals thrown in. The same is the case with humans. But where might we look to find that which gives we humans *objective* value?

No more likely candidate exists apart from God.

But what evidence is there that God values us at all? Well, on this view, our mere existence speaks to some kind of value. If we had no value at all, we simply wouldn't exist. But this kind of valuing doesn't stir the heart much. For that kind of stirring, we must look to examples from our experience that have left an impact on us the most. I am thinking of the soldier who throws himself on a grenade to save the lives of his brothers in the foxhole. Or, the parent working night and day to put food on the table for the children. One sacrifices oneself only for the things they value- yet all this is ultimately meaningless if we are just dollars floating around with no one to treat us as 'currency.'

Only Christianity has the answer.

In Christianity, God himself revealed in vivid detail how much the human race is valued. It is said that humans are made in His image. This well explains our disgust at injustice and bloodshed and pervasive desire to do 'good,' or at least wrap up whatever we're doing in a justification that looks 'good.' Yet if all we had was this claim it would not be enough. If God had not backed it up in any tangible way, one might possibly regard it as a mere abstraction.

Only in Christianity is it claimed that, as a real fact, God put his money where his mouth was in regards to his valuing of humans. He came to earth as a man. He moved among us for a time, proving to everyone He interacted with at the time that He was who He said He was. He did this before both friend and foe, though it doesn't follow that simply because a proof was provided that it was accepted. Finally, his foes executed him, stapling him to planks of wood. An innocent man was slaughtered to appease the political and national aspirations of a few. An injustice was carried out, and blood ran down all over the place.

So it is that Christianity says that God himself suffered for us. He came to die for us, and be a sacrifice for us. The story goes on, though: it was all a great rescue mission. God was victorious! Death itself was defeated, and the way was opened for the whole human race to have life, and life to the fullest. In light of the fact that God paid for us all in blood, let no man say that we are not special, that we have no intrinsic value relative to each other, that we are mere beasts.

The pivot of civilization turns out to be a person, bloodied up and put to death for the sake of all.

As it happens, everything ultimately pivots on how we regard this person and this event. The history of the 20th century shows what happens when a great mass of individuals dispenses with Jesus and his death and resurrection as mere superstition and attempts to raise up their own Tower of Civilization on their own power, strength, and wisdom. Are we quite sure that the history of the 21st century will be any different if we proceed along the same lines, even with the Holocaust and communist purges still in sight in our rear view mirror?

The question must be faced bravely. If this means one must examine the claims of Christ and Christianity more closely, then the brave person will certainly do so. If these claims be rejected, do not cease to be brave: pick up Sanger's task and do not be unashamed of doing so. Do not hide it in verbiage and innuendo and strained attempts to label what you're doing as some kind of 'objective' good. We all know that on your conclusions there can be no such thing.

And yet... and yet... there is still that repulsion you can't escape... it still requires explanation... some firm basis... It isn't because you are a coward that you reject genocide... there seems to be something more to it. You really are brave? Then don't regard the only worldview that can actually explain such revulsion- Christianity- with prejudice and arrogance. Don't reject it only because there are other implications that you don't like.

And don't refuse to examine it simply because you are chicken.

For further research:

Eugenics and Other Evils. By G. K. Chesterton.
Maafa21 (a documentary) by Life Dynamics.

Anthony Horvath is a Christian apologist, writer, and pro-life speaker. He and his wife were given the 'option' to kill their daughter, diagnosed at the 20 week ultrasound with the condition spina bifida. They emphatically rejected this 'option.' Their daughter continues to show the world just how valuable she is and how much value she adds to those she loves- which is everyone.
Learn more at www.wechoselife.com.

> It is better for all the world if, instead of waiting to execute degenerate offspring for crime, or to let them starve for their imbecility, society can prevent those who are manifestly unfit from continuing their kind. The principle that sustains compulsory vaccination is broad enough to cover cutting the Fallopian tubes. Three generations of imbeciles are enough.
>
> Oliver Wendell Holmes
> Supreme Court Chief Justice
> Buck vs Bell, 1927

A Plan for Peace
by Margaret Sanger
1932

First, put into action President Wilson's fourteen points, upon which terms Germany and Austria surrendered to the Allies in 1918.

Second, have Congress set up a special department for the study of population problems and appoint a Parliament of Population, the directors representing the various branches of science: this body to direct and control the population through birth rates and immigration, and to direct its distribution over the country according to national needs consistent with taste, fitness and interest of individuals. The main objects of the Population Congress would be:

a. to raise the level and increase the general intelligence of population.

b. to increase the population slowly by keeping the birth rate at its present level of fifteen per thousand, decreasing the death rate below its present mark of 11 per thousand.

c. to keep the doors of immigration closed to the entrance of certain aliens whose condition is known to be detrimental to the stamina of the race, such as feebleminded, idiots, morons, insane, syphilitic, epileptic, criminal, professional prostitutes, and others in this class barred by the immigration laws of 1924.

d. to apply a stern and rigid policy of sterilization and segregation to that grade of population whose progeny is tainted, or whose inheritance is such that objectionable traits may be transmitted to offspring.

e. to insure the country against future burdens of maintenance for numerous offspring as may be born of feebleminded parents, by pensioning all persons with transmissible disease who voluntarily consent to sterilization.

f. to give certain dysgenic groups in our population their choice of segregation or sterilization.

g. to apportion farm lands and homesteads for these segregated persons where they would be taught to work under competent instructors for the period of their entire lives.

The first step would thus be to control the intake and output of morons, mental defectives, epileptics.

The second step would be to take an inventory of the secondary group such as illiterates, paupers, unemployables, criminals, prostitutes, dope-fiends; classify them in special departments under government medical protection, and segregate them on farms and open spaces as long as necessary for the strengthening and development of moral conduct.

Having corralled this enormous part of our population and placed it on a basis of health instead of punishment, it is safe to say that fifteen or twenty millions of our population would then be organized into soldiers of defense—defending the unborn against their own disabilities.

The third step would be to give special attention to the mothers' health, to see that women who are suffering from tuberculosis, heart or kidney disease, toxic goiter, gonorrhea, or any disease where the condition of pregnancy disturbs their health are placed under public health nurses to instruct them in practical, scientific methods of contraception in order to safeguard their lives—thus reducing maternal mortality.

The above steps may seem to place emphasis on a health program instead of on tariffs, moratoriums and debts, but I believe that national health is the first essential factor in any program for universal peace.

With the future citizen safeguarded from hereditary taints, with five million mental and moral degenerates segregated, with ten million women and ten million children receiving adequate care, we could then turn our attention to the basic needs for international peace.

There would then be a definite effort to make population increase slowly and at a specified rate, in order to accommodate and adjust increasing numbers to the best social and economic system.

In the meantime we should organize and join an International League of Low Birth Rate Nations to secure and maintain World Peace.

Summary of address before the New History Society, January 17th, New York City. Published in Birth Control Review (April 1932, pp. 107-108).

Margaret Sanger's Dedication

to *The Pivot of Civilization*:

To Alice Drysdale Vickery

Whose prophetic vision of liberated womanhood has been an inspiration

"I dream of a world in which the spirits of women are flames stronger than fire, a world in which modesty has become courage and yet remains modesty, a world in which women are as unlike men as ever they were in the world I sought to destroy, a world in which women shine with a loveliness of self-revelation as enchanting as ever the old legends told, and yet a world which would immeasurably transcend the old world in the self-sacrificing passion of human service. I have dreamed of that world ever since I began to dream at all."
—Havelock Ellis

INTRODUCTION

Birth Control, Mrs. Sanger claims, and claims rightly, to be a question of fundamental importance at the present time. I do not know how far one is justified in calling it the pivot or the corner-stone of a progressive civilization. These terms involve a criticism of metaphors that may take us far away from the question in hand. Birth Control is no new thing in human experience, and it has been practised in societies of the most various types and fortunes. But there can be little doubt that at the present time it is a test issue between two widely different interpretations of the word civilization, and of what is good in life and conduct. The way in which men and women range themselves in this controversy is more simply and directly indicative of their general intellectual quality than any other single indication. I do not wish to imply by this that the people who oppose are more or less intellectual than the people who advocate Birth Control, but only that they have fundamentally contrasted general ideas,—that, mentally, they are *different*. Very simple, very complex, very dull and very brilliant persons may be found in either camp, but all those in either camp have certain attitudes in common which they share with one another, and do not share with those in the other camp.

There have been many definitions of civilization. Civilization is a complexity of countless aspects, and may be validly defined in a great number of relationships. A reader of James Harvey Robinson's MIND IN THE MAKING will find it very reasonable to define a civilization as a system of society-making ideas at issue with reality. Just so far as the system of ideas meets the needs and conditions of survival or is able to adapt itself to the needs and conditions of survival of the society it dominates, so far will that society continue and prosper. We are beginning to realize that in the past and under different conditions from our own, societies have existed with systems of ideas and with methods of thought very widely contrasting with what we should consider right and sane to-day. The extraordinary neolithic civilizations of the American continent that flourished before the coming of the Europeans, seem to have got along with concepts that involved pedantries and cruelties and a kind of systematic unreason, which find their closest parallels to-day in the art and writings of certain types of lunatic. There are collections of drawings from English and American asylums extraordinarily parallel in their spirit and quality with the Maya inscriptions of Central America. Yet these neolithic American societies got along for hundreds and perhaps thousands of years, they respected seed-time and harvest, they bred and they maintained a grotesque and terrible order. And they produced quite beautiful works of art. Yet their surplus of population was disposed of by an organization of sacrificial slaughter unparalleled in the records of mankind. Many of the institutions that seemed most normal and respectable to them, filled the invading Europeans with perplexity and horror.

When we realize clearly this possibility of civilizations being based on very different sets of moral ideas and upon different intellectual methods, we are better able to appreciate the profound significance of the schism in our modern community, which gives us side by side, honest and intelligent people who regard Birth Control as something essentially sweet, sane, clean, desirable and necessary, and others equally honest and with as good a claim to intelligence who regard it as not merely unreasonable and unwholesome, but as intolerable and abominable. We are living not in a simple and complete civilization, but in a conflict of at least two civilizations, based on entirely different fundamental ideas, pursuing different methods and with different aims and ends.

I will call one of these civilizations our Traditional or Authoritative Civilization. It rests upon the thing that is, and upon the thing that has been. It insists upon respect for custom and usage; it discourages criticism and enquiry. It is very ancient and conservative, or, going beyond conservation, it is reactionary. The vehement hostility of many Catholic priests and prelates towards new views of human origins, and new views of moral questions, has led many careless thinkers to identify this old traditional civilization with Christianity, but that identification ignores the strongly revolutionary and initiatory spirit that has always animated Christianity, and is untrue even to the realities of orthodox Catholic teaching. The vituperation of individual Catholics must not be confused with the deliberate doctrines of the Church which have, on the whole, been conspicuously cautious and balanced and sane in these matters. The ideas and practices of the Old Civilization are older and more widespread than and not identifiable with either Christian or Catholic culture, and it will be a great misfortune if the issues between the Old Civilization and the New are allowed to slip into the deep ruts of religious controversies that are only accidentally and intermittently parallel.

Contrasted with the ancient civilization, with the Traditional disposition, which accepts institutions and moral values as though they were a part of nature, we have what I may call—with an evident bias in its favour—the civilization of enquiry, of experimental knowledge, Creative and Progressive Civilization. The first great outbreak of the spirit of this civilization was in republican Greece; the martyrdom of Socrates, the fearless Utopianism of Plato, the ambitious encyclopaedism of Aristotle, mark the dawn of a new courage and a new wilfulness in human affairs. The fear of set limitations, of punitive and restrictive laws imposed by Fate upon human life was visibly fading in human minds. These names mark the first clear realization that to a large extent, and possibly to an illimitable extent, man's moral and social life and his general destiny could be seized upon and controlled by man. But—he must have knowledge. Said the Ancient Civilization—and it says it still through a multitude of vigorous voices and harsh repressive acts: "Let man learn his duty and obey." Says the New Civilization, with ever-increasing confidence: "Let man know, and trust him."

For long ages, the Old Civilization kept the New subordinate, apologetic and ineffective, but for the last two centuries, the New has fought its way to a position of contentious equality. The two go on side by side, jostling upon a thousand issues. The world changes, the conditions of life change rapidly, through that development of organized science which is the natural method of the New Civilization. The old tradition demands that national loyalties and ancient belligerence should continue. The new has produced means of communication that break down the pens and separations of human life upon which nationalist emotion depends. The old tradition insists upon its ancient blood-letting of war; the new knowledge carries that war to undreamt of levels of destruction. The ancient system needed an unrestricted breeding to meet the normal waste of life through war, pestilence, and a multitude of hitherto unpreventable diseases. The new knowledge sweeps away the venerable checks of pestilence and disease, and confronts us with the congestions and explosive dangers of an over-populated world. The old tradition demands a special prolific class doomed to labor and subservience; the new points to mechanism and to scientific organization as a means of escape from this immemorial subjugation. Upon every main issue in life, there is this quarrel between the method of submission and the method of knowledge. More and more do men of science and intelligent people generally realize the hopelessness of pouring new wine into old bottles. More and more clearly do they grasp the significance of the Great Teacher's parable.

The New Civilization is saying to the Old now: "We cannot go on making power for you to spend upon international conflict. You must stop waving flags and bandying insults. You must organize the Peace of the World; you must subdue yourselves to the Federation of all mankind. And we cannot go on giving you health, freedom, enlargement, limitless wealth, if all our gifts to you are to be swamped by an indiscriminate torrent of progeny. We want fewer and better children who can be reared up to their full possibilities in unencumbered homes, and we cannot make the social life and the world-peace we are determined to make, with the ill-bred, ill-trained swarms of inferior citizens that you inflict upon us." And there at the passionate and crucial question, this essential and fundamental question, whether procreation is still to be a superstitious and often disastrous mystery, undertaken in fear and ignorance, reluctantly and under the sway of blind desires, or whether it is to become a deliberate creative act, the two civilizations join issue now. It is a conflict from which it is almost impossible to abstain. Our acts, our way of living, our social tolerance, our very silences will count in this crucial decision between the old and the new.

In a plain and lucid style without any emotional appeals, Mrs. Margaret Sanger sets out the case of the new order against the old. There have been several able books published recently upon the question of Birth Control, from the point of view of a woman's personal life, and from the point of view of married happiness, but I do not think there has been any book as yet, popularly accessible, which presents this matter from the point of view of the public good, and as a necessary step to the further improvement of human life as a whole. I am inclined to think that there has hitherto been rather too much personal emotion spent upon this business and far too little attention given to its broader aspects. Mrs. Sanger with her extraordinary breadth of outlook and the real scientific quality of her mind, has now redressed the balance. She has lifted this question from out of the warm atmosphere of troubled domesticity in which it has hitherto been discussed, to its proper level of a predominantly important human affair.

H.G. Wells
Easton Glebe,
Dunmow,
Essex.,
England

THE PIVOT OF CIVILIZATION

CHAPTER I: A New Truth Emerges

Be not ashamed, women, your privilege encloses the
rest, and is the exit of the rest,
You are the gates of the body, and you are the gates of the soul.

—Walt Whitman

This book aims to be neither the first word on the tangled problems of human society to-day, nor the last. My aim has been to emphasize, by the use of concrete and challenging examples and neglected facts, the need of a new approach to individual and social problems. Its central challenge is that civilization, in any true sense of the word, is based upon the control and guidance of the great natural instinct of Sex. Mastery of this force is possible only through the instrument of Birth Control.

It may be objected that in the following pages I have rushed in where academic scholars have feared to tread, and that as an active propagandist I am lacking in the scholarship and documentary preparation to undertake such a stupendous task. My only defense is that, from my point of view at least, too many are already studying and investigating social problems from without, with a sort of Olympian detachment. And on the other hand, too few of those who are engaged in this endless war for human betterment have found the time to give to the world those truths not always hidden but practically unquarried, which may be secured only after years of active service.

Of late, we have been treated to accounts written by well-meaning ladies and gentlemen who have assumed clever disguises and have gone out to work—for a week or a month—among the proletariat. But can we thus learn anything new of the fundamental problems of working men, working women, working children? Something, perhaps, but not those great central problems of Hunger and Sex. We have been told that only those who themselves have suffered the pangs of starvation can truly understand Hunger. You might come into the closest contact with a starving man; yet, if you were yourself well-fed, no amount of sympathy could give you actual insight into the psychology of his suffering. This suggests an objective and a subjective approach to all social problems. Whatever the weakness of the subjective (or, if you prefer, the feminine) approach, it has at least the virtue that its conclusions are tested by experience. Observation of facts about you, intimate subjective reaction to such facts, generate in your mind certain fundamental

1

convictions,—truths you can ignore no more than you can ignore such truths as come as the fruit of bitter but valuable personal experience.

Regarding myself, I may say that my experience in the course of the past twelve or fifteen years has been of a type to force upon me certain convictions that demand expression. For years I had believed that the solution of all our troubles was to be found in well-defined programmes of political and legislative action. At first, I concentrated my whole attention upon these, only to discover that politicians and law-makers are just as confused and as much at a loss in solving fundamental problems as anyone else. And I am speaking here not so much of the corrupt and ignorant politician as of those idealists and reformers who think that by the ballot society may be led to an earthly paradise. They may honestly desire and intend to do great things. They may positively glow—before election—with enthusiasm at the prospect they imagine political victory may open to them. Time after time, I was struck by the change in their attitude after the briefest enjoyment of this illusory power. Men are elected during some wave of reform, let us say, elected to legislate into practical working existence some great ideal. They want to do big things; but a short time in office is enough to show the political idealist that he can accomplish nothing, that his reform must be debased and dragged into the dust, so that even if it becomes enacted, it may be not merely of no benefit, but a positive evil. It is scarcely necessary to emphasize this point. It is an accepted commonplace of American politics. So much of life, so large a part of all our social problems, moreover, remains untouched by political and legislative action. This is an old truth too often ignored by those who plan political campaigns upon the most superficial knowledge of human nature.

My own eyes were opened to the limitations of political action when, as an organizer for a political group in New York, I attended by chance a meeting of women laundry-workers who were on strike. We believed we could help these women with a legislative measure and asked their support. "Oh! that stuff!" exclaimed one of these women. "Don't you know that we women might be dead and buried if we waited for politicians and lawmakers to right our wrongs?" This set me to thinking—not merely of the immediate problem—but to asking myself how much any male politician could understand of the wrongs inflicted upon poor working women.

I threw the weight of my study and activity into the economic and industrial struggle. Here I discovered men and women fired with the glorious vision of a new world, of a proletarian world emancipated, a Utopian world,—it glowed in romantic colours for the majority of those with whom I came in closest contact. The next step, the immediate step, was another matter, less romantic and too often less encouraging. In their ardor, some of the labor leaders of that period almost convinced us that the millennium was just around the corner. Those were the pre-war days of dramatic strikes. But even when most under the spell of the new vision, the sight of the overburdened wives of the strikers, with their puny babies and their broods of under-fed children, made us stop and think of a neglected factor in the march toward our earthly paradise. It was well enough to ask the poor men workers to carry on the battle against economic injustice. But what results could be expected when they were forced in addition to carry the burden of their ever-growing families? This question loomed large to those of us who came into intimate contact with the women and children. We saw that in the final analysis the real burden of economic and industrial warfare was thrust upon the frail, all-too-frail shoulders of the children, the very babies—the coming generation. In their wan faces, in their undernourished bodies, would be indelibly written the bitter defeat of their parents.

The eloquence of those who led the underpaid and half-starved workers could no longer, for me, at least, ring with conviction. Something more than the purely economic interpretation was involved. The bitter struggle for bread, for a home and material comfort, was but one phase of the problem. There was another phase, perhaps even more fundamental, that had been absolutely neglected by the adherents of the new dogmas. That other phase was the driving power of instinct, a power uncontrolled and unnoticed. The great fundamental instinct of sex was expressing itself in these ever-growing broods, in the prosperity of the slum midwife and her colleague the slum undertaker. In spite of all my sympathy with the dream of liberated Labor, I was driven to ask whether this urging power of sex, this deep instinct, was not at least partially responsible, along with industrial injustice, for the widespread misery of the world.

To find an answer to this problem which at that point in my experience I could not solve, I determined to study conditions in Europe. Perhaps there I might discover a new approach, a great illumination. Just before the outbreak of the war, I visited France, Spain, Germany and Great Britain. Everywhere I found the same dogmas and prejudices among labor leaders, the same intense but limited vision, the same insistence upon the purely economic phases of human nature, the same belief that if the problem of hunger were solved, the question of the women and children would take care of itself. In this attitude I discovered, then, what seemed to me to be purely masculine reasoning; and because it was purely masculine, it could at best be but half true. Feminine insight must be brought to bear on all questions; and here, it struck me, the fallacy of the masculine, the all-too-masculine, was brutally exposed. I was encouraged and strengthened in this attitude by the support of certain leaders who had studied human nature and who had reached the same conclusion: that civilization could not solve the problem of Hunger until it recognized the titanic strength of the sexual instinct. In Spain, I found that Lorenzo Portet, who was carrying on the work of the martyred Francisco Ferrer, had reached this same conclusion. In Italy, Enrico Malatesta, the valiant leader who was after the war to play so dramatic a role, was likewise combating the current dogma of the orthodox Socialists. In Berlin, Rudolph Rocker was engaged in the thankless task of puncturing the articles of faith of the orthodox Marxian religion. It is quite needless to add that these men who had probed beneath the surface of the problem and had diagnosed so much more completely the complex malady of contemporary society were intensely disliked by the superficial theorists of the neo-Marxian School.

The gospel of Marx had, however, been too long and too thoroughly inculcated into the minds of millions of workers in Europe, to be discarded. It is a flattering doctrine, since it teaches the laborer that all the fault is with someone else, that he is the victim of circumstances, and not even a partner in the creation of his own and his child's misery. Not without significance was the additional discovery that I made. I found that the Marxian influence tended to lead workers to believe that, irrespective of the health of the poor mothers, the earning capacity of the wage-earning fathers, or the upbringing of the children, increase of the proletarian family was a benefit, not a detriment to the revolutionary movement. The greater the number of hungry mouths, the emptier the stomachs, the more quickly would the "Class War" be precipitated. The greater the increase in population among the proletariat, the greater the incentive to revolution. This may not be sound Marxian theory; but it is the manner in which it is popularly accepted. It is the popular belief, wherever the Marxian influence is strong. This I found especially in England and Scotland. In speaking to groups of dockworkers on strike in Glasgow, and before the communist and co-operative guilds throughout England, I discovered a prevailing opposition to the recognition of sex as a factor in the perpetuation of poverty. The leaders and theorists were immovable in their opposition. But when once I succeeded in breaking through the surface opposition of the rank and file of the workers, I found that they were willing to recognize the power of this neglected factor in their lives.

So central, so fundamental in the life of every man and woman is this problem that they need be taught no elaborate or imposing theory to explain their troubles. To approach their problems by the avenue of sex and reproduction is to reveal at once their fundamental relations to the whole economic and biological structure of society. Their interest is immediately and completely awakened. But always, as I soon discovered, the ideas and habits of thought of these submerged masses have been formed through the Press, the Church, through political institutions, all of which had built up a conspiracy of silence around a subject that is of no less vital importance than that of Hunger. A great wall separates the masses from those imperative truths that must be known and flung wide if civilization is to be saved. As currently constituted, Church, Press, Education seem to-day organized to exploit the ignorance and the prejudices of the masses, rather than to light their way to self-salvation.

Such was the situation in 1914, when I returned to America, determined, since the exclusively masculine point of view had dominated too long, that the other half of the truth should be made known. The Birth Control movement was launched because it was in this form that the whole relation of woman

4

and child—eternal emblem of the future of society—could be more effectively dramatized. The amazing growth of this movement dates from the moment when in my home a small group organized the first Birth Control League. Since then we have been criticized for our choice of the term "Birth Control" to express the idea of modern scientific contraception. I have yet to hear any criticism of this term that is not based upon some false and hypocritical sense of modesty, or that does not arise out of a semi-prurient misunderstanding of its aim. On the other hand: nothing better expresses the idea of purposive, responsible, and self-directed guidance of the reproductive powers.

Those critics who condemn Birth Control as a negative, destructive idea, concerned only with self-gratification, might profitably open the nearest dictionary for a definition of "control." There they would discover that the verb "control" means to exercise a directing, guiding, or restraining influence;—to direct, to regulate, to counteract. Control is guidance, direction, foresight. It implies intelligence, forethought and responsibility. They will find in the Standard Dictionary a quotation from Lecky to the effect that, "The greatest of all evils in politics is power without control." In what phase of life is not "power without control" an evil? Birth Control, therefore, means not merely the limitation of births, but the application of intelligent guidance over the reproductive power. It means the substitution of reason and intelligence for the blind play of instinct.

The term "Birth Control" had the immense practical advantage of compressing into two short words the answer to the inarticulate demands of millions of men and women in all countries. At the time this slogan was formulated, I had not yet come to the complete realization of the great truth that had been thus crystallized. It was the response to the overwhelming, heart-breaking appeals that came by every mail for aid and advice, which revealed a great truth that lay dormant, a truth that seemed to spring into full vitality almost over night—that could never again be crushed to earth!

Nor could I then have realized the number and the power of the enemies who were to be aroused into activity by this idea. So completely was I dominated by this conviction of the efficacy of "control," that I could not until later realize the extent of the sacrifices that were to be exacted of me and of those who supported my campaign. The very idea of Birth Control resurrected the spirit of the witch-hunters of Salem. Could they have usurped the power, they would have burned us at the stake. Lacking that power, they used the weapon of suppression, and invoked medieval statutes to send us to jail. These tactics had an effect the very opposite to that intended. They demonstrated the vitality of the idea of Birth Control, and acted as counter-irritant on the actively intelligent sections of the American community. Nor was the interest aroused confined merely to America. The neo-Malthusian movement in Great Britain with its history of undaunted bravery, came to our support; and I had the comfort of knowing that the finest minds of England did not hesitate a moment in the expression of their sympathy and support.

In America, on the other hand, I found from the beginning until very recently that the so-called intellectuals exhibited a curious and almost inexplicable reticence in supporting Birth Control. They even hesitated to voice any public protest against the campaign to crush us which was inaugurated and sustained by the most reactionary and sinister forces in American life. It was not inertia or any lack of interest on the part of the masses that stood in our way. It was the indifference of the intellectual leaders.

Writers, teachers, ministers, editors, who form a class dictating, if not creating, public opinion, are, in this country, singularly inhibited or unconscious of their true function in the community. One of their first duties, it is certain, should be to champion the constitutional right of free speech and free press, to welcome any idea that tends to awaken the critical attention of the great American public. But those who reveal themselves as fully cognizant of this public duty are in the minority, and must possess more than average courage to survive the enmity such an attitude provokes.

One of the chief aims of the present volume is to stimulate American intellectuals to abandon the mental habits which prevent them from seeing human nature as a whole, instead of as something that can be pigeonholed into various compartments or classes. Birth Control affords an approach to the study of humanity because it cuts through the limitations of current methods. It is economic, biological, psychological and spiritual in its aspects. It awakens the vision of mankind moving and changing, of humanity growing and developing, coming to fruition, of a race creative, flowering into beautiful expression through talent and genius.

As a social programme, Birth Control is not merely concerned with population questions. In this respect, it is a distinct step in advance of earlier Malthusian doctrines, which concerned themselves chiefly with economics and population. Birth Control concerns itself with the spirit no less than the body. It looks for the liberation of the spirit of woman and through woman of the child. To-day motherhood is wasted, penalized, tortured. Children brought into the world by unwilling mothers suffer an initial handicap that cannot be measured by cold statistics. Their lives are blighted from the start. To substantiate this fact, I have chosen to present the conclusions of reports on Child Labor and records of defect and delinquency published by organizations with no bias in favour of Birth Control. The evidence is before us. It crowds in upon us from all sides. But prior to this new approach, no attempt had been made to correlate the effects of the blind and irresponsible play of the sexual instinct with its deep-rooted causes.

The duty of the educator and the intellectual creator of public opinion is, in this connection, of the greatest importance. For centuries official moralists, priests, clergymen and teachers, statesmen and politicians have preached the doctrine of glorious and divine fertility. To-day, we are confronted with the world-wide spectacle of the realization of this doctrine. It is not without significance that the moron and the imbecile set the pace in living up to this teaching, and that the intellectuals, the educators, the archbishops, bishops, priests, who are most insistent on it, are the staunchest adherents in their own lives of celibacy and non-fertility. It is time to point out to the champions of unceasing and indiscriminate fertility the results of their teaching.

One of the greatest difficulties in giving to the public a book of this type is the impossibility of keeping pace with the events and changes of a movement that is now, throughout the world, striking root and growing. The changed attitude of the American Press indicates that enlightened public opinion no longer tolerates a policy of silence upon a question of the most vital importance. Almost simultaneously in England and America, two incidents have broken through the prejudice and the guarded silence of centuries. At the church Congress in Birmingham, October 12, 1921, Lord Dawson, the king's physician, in criticizing the report of the Lambeth Conference concerning Birth Control, delivered an address defending this practice. Of such bravery and eloquence that it could not be ignored, this address electrified the entire British public. It aroused a storm of abuse, and yet succeeded, as no propaganda could, in mobilizing the forces of progress and intelligence in the support of the cause.

Just one month later, the First American Birth Control Conference culminated in a significant and dramatic incident. At the close of the conference a mass meeting was scheduled in the Town Hall, New York City, to discuss the morality of Birth Control. Mr. Harold Cox, editor of the *Edinburgh Review*, who had come to New York to attend the conference, was to lead the discussion. It seemed only natural for us to call together scientists, educators, members of the medical profession, and theologians of all denominations, to ask their opinion upon this uncertain and important phase of the controversy. Letters were sent to eminent men and women in different parts of the world. In this letter we asked the following questions:—

1. Is over-population a menace to the peace of the world?

2. Would the legal dissemination of scientific Birth Control information, through the medium of clinics by the medical profession, be the most logical method of checking the problem of over-population?

3. Would knowledge of Birth Control change the moral attitude of men and women toward the marriage bond, or lower the moral standards of the youth of the country?

4. Do you believe that knowledge which enables parents to limit their families will make for human happiness, and raise the moral, social and intellectual standards of population?

We sent this questionnaire not only to those who we thought might agree with us, but we sent it also to our known opponents.

When I arrived at the Town Hall the entrance was guarded by policemen. They told me there would be no meeting. Before my arrival our executives had been greeted by Monsignor Dineen, secretary of Archbishop Hayes, of the Roman Catholic archdiocese, who informed them that the meeting would be prohibited on the ground that it was contrary to public morals. The police had closed the doors. When they opened them to permit the exit of the large audience which had gathered, Mr. Cox and I entered. I attempted to exercise my constitutional right of free speech, but was prohibited and arrested. Miss Mary Winsor, who protested against this unwarranted arrest, was likewise dragged off to the police station. The case was dismissed the following morning. The ecclesiastic instigators of the affair were conspicuous by their absence from the police court. But the incident was enough to expose the opponents of Birth Control and the extreme methods they used to combat our progress. The case was too flagrant, too gross an affront, to pass unnoticed by the newspapers. The progress of our movement was indicated in the changed attitude of the American Press, which had perceived the danger to the public of the unlawful tactics used by the enemies of Birth Control in preventing open discussion of a vital question.

No social idea has inspired its advocates with more bravery, tenacity, and courage than Birth Control. From the early days of Francis Place and Richard Carlile, to those of the Drysdales and Edward Trulove, of Bradlaugh and Mrs. Annie Besant, its advocates have faced imprisonment and ostracism. In the whole history of the English movement, there has been no more courageous figure than that of the venerable Alice Drysdale Vickery, the undaunted torch-bearer who has bridged the silence of forty-four years—since the Bradlaugh-Besant trial. She stands head and shoulders above the professional feminists. Serenely has she withstood jeers and jests. To-day, she continues to point out to the younger generation which is devoted to newer palliatives the fundamental relation between Sex and Hunger.

The First American Birth Control Conference, held at the same time as the Washington Conference for the Limitation of Armaments, marks a turning-point in our approach to social problems. The Conference made evident the fact that in every field of scientific and social endeavour the most penetrating thinkers are now turning to the consideration of our problem as a fundamental necessity to American civilization. They are coming to see that a *qualitative* factor as opposed to a *quantitative* one is of primary importance in dealing with the great masses of humanity.

Certain fundamental convictions should be made clear here. The programme for Birth Control is not a charity. It is not aiming to interfere in the private lives of poor people, to tell them how many children they should have, nor to sit in judgment upon their fitness to become parents. It aims, rather, to awaken responsibility, to answer the demand for a scientific means by which and through which each human life may be self-directed and self-controlled. The exponent of Birth Control, in short, is convinced that social

8

regeneration, no less than individual regeneration, must come from within. Every potential parent, and especially every potential mother, must be brought to an acute realization of the primary and individual responsibility of bringing children into this world. Not until the parents of this world are given control over their reproductive faculties will it be possible to improve the quality of the generations of the future, or even to maintain civilization at its present level. Only when given intelligent mastery of the procreative powers can the great mass of humanity be aroused to a realization of responsibility of parenthood. We have come to the conclusion, based on widespread investigation and experience, that education for parenthood must be based upon the needs and demands of the people themselves. An idealistic code of sexual ethics, imposed from above, a set of rules devised by high-minded theorists who fail to take into account the living conditions and desires of the masses, can never be of the slightest value in effecting change in the customs of the people. Systems so imposed in the past have revealed their woeful inability to prevent the sexual and racial chaos into which the world has drifted.

The universal demand for practical education in Birth Control is one of the most hopeful signs that the masses themselves to-day possess the divine spark of regeneration. It remains for the courageous and the enlightened to answer this demand, to kindle the spark, to direct a thorough education in sex hygiene based upon this intense interest.

Birth Control is thus the entering wedge for the educator. In answering the needs of these thousands upon thousands of submerged mothers, it is possible to use their interest as the foundation for education in prophylaxis, hygiene and infant welfare. The potential mother can then be shown that maternity need not be slavery but may be the most effective avenue to self-development and self-realization. Upon this basis only may we improve the quality of the race.

The lack of balance between the birth-rate of the "unfit" and the "fit," admittedly the greatest present menace to the civilization, can never be rectified by the inauguration of a cradle competition between these two classes. The example of the inferior classes, the fertility of the feeble-minded, the mentally defective, the poverty-stricken, should not be held up for emulation to the mentally and physically fit, and therefore less fertile, parents of the educated and well-to-do classes. On the contrary, the most urgent problem to-day is how to limit and discourage the over-fertility of the mentally and physically defective. Possibly drastic and Spartan methods may be forced upon American society if it continues complacently to encourage the chance and chaotic breeding that has resulted from our stupid, cruel sentimentalism.

To effect the salvation of the generations of the future—nay, of the generations of to-day—our greatest need, first of all, is the ability to face the situation without flinching; to cooperate in the formation of a code of sexual ethics based upon a thorough biological and psychological understanding of human nature; and then to answer the questions and the needs of the people with all the intelligence and honesty at our command. If we can summon the bravery to do this, we shall best be serving the pivotal interests of civilization.

To conclude this introduction: my initiation, as I have confessed, was primarily an emotional one. My interest in Birth Control was awakened by experience. Research and investigation have followed. Our effort has been to raise our program from the plane of the emotional to the plane of the scientific. Any social progress, it is my belief, must purge itself of sentimentalism and pass through the crucible of science. We are willing to submit Birth Control to this test. It is part of the purpose of this book to appeal to the scientist for aid, to arouse that interest which will result in widespread research and investigation. I believe that my personal experience with this idea must be that of the race at large. We must temper our emotion and enthusiasm with the impersonal determination of science. We must unite in the task of creating an instrument of steel, strong but supple, if we are to triumph finally in the war for human emancipation.

CHAPTER II: Conscripted Motherhood

"Their poor, old ravaged and stiffened faces, their poor, old bodies dried up with ceaseless toil, their patient souls made me weep. They are our conscripts. They are the venerable ones whom we should reverence. All the mystery of womanhood seems incarnated in their ugly being—the Mothers! the Mothers! Ye are all one!"

—From the Letters of William James

Motherhood, which is not only the oldest but the most important profession in the world, has received few of the benefits of civilization. It is a curious fact that a civilization devoted to mother-worship, that publicly professes a worship of mother and child, should close its eyes to the appalling waste of human life and human energy resulting from those dire consequences of leaving the whole problem of child-bearing to chance and blind instinct. It would be untrue to say that among the civilized nations of the world to-day, the profession of motherhood remains in a barbarous state. The bitter truth is that motherhood, among the larger part of our population, does not rise to the level of the barbarous or the primitive. Conditions of life among the primitive tribes were rude enough and severe enough to prevent the unhealthy growth of sentimentality, and to discourage the irresponsible production of defective children. Moreover, there is ample evidence to indicate that even among the most primitive peoples the function of maternity was recognized as of primary and central importance to the community.

If we define civilization as increased and increasing responsibility based on vision and foresight, it becomes painfully evident that the profession of motherhood as practised to-day is in no sense civilized. Educated people derive their ideas of maternity for the most part, either from the experience of their own set, or from visits to impressive hospitals where women of the upper classes receive the advantages of modern science and modern nursing. From these charming pictures they derive their complacent views of the beauty of motherhood and their confidence for the future of the race. The other side of the picture is revealed only to the trained investigator, to the patient and impartial observer who visits not merely one or two "homes of the poor," but makes detailed studies of town after town, obtains the history of each mother, and finally correlates and analyzes this evidence. Upon such a basis are we able to draw conclusions concerning this strange business of bringing children into the world.

Every year I receive thousands of letters from women in all parts of America, desperate appeals to aid them to extricate themselves from the trap of compulsory maternity. Lest I be accused of bias and exaggeration in drawing my conclusions from these painful human documents, I prefer to present a number of typical cases recorded in the reports of the United States

Government, and in the evidence of trained and impartial investigators of social agencies more generally opposed to the doctrine of Birth Control than biased in favor of it.

A perusal of the reports on infant mortality in widely varying industrial centers of the United States, published during the past decade by the Children's Bureau of the United States Department of Labor, forces us to a realization of the immediate need of detailed statistics concerning the practice and results of uncontrolled breeding. Some such effort as this has been made by the Galton Laboratory of National Eugenics in Great Britain. The Children's Bureau reports only incidentally present this impressive evidence. They fail to coordinate it. While there is always the danger of drawing giant conclusions from pigmy premises, here is overwhelming evidence concerning irresponsible parenthood that is ignored by governmental and social agencies.

I have chosen a small number of typical cases from these reports. Though drawn from widely varying sources, they all emphasize the greatest crime of modern civilization—that of permitting motherhood to be left to blind chance, and to be mainly a function of the most abysmally ignorant and irresponsible classes of the community.

Here is a fairly typical case from Johnstown, Pennsylvania. A woman of thirty-eight years had undergone thirteen pregnancies in seventeen years. Of eleven live births and two premature stillbirths, only two children were alive at the time of the government agent's visit. The second to eighth, the eleventh and the thirteenth had died of bowel trouble, at ages ranging from three weeks to four months. The only cause of these deaths the mother could give was that "food did not agree with them." She confessed quite frankly that she believed in feeding babies, and gave them everything anybody told her to give them. She began to give them at the age of one month, bread, potatoes, egg, crackers, etc. For the last baby that died, this mother had bought a goat and gave its milk to the baby; the goat got sick, but the mother continued to give her baby its milk until the goat went dry. Moreover, she directed the feeding of her daughter's baby until it died at the age of three months. "On account of the many children she had had, the neighbors consider her an authority on baby care."

Lest this case be considered too tragically ridiculous to be accepted as typical, the reader may verify it with an almost interminable list of similar cases.[1] Parental irresponsibility is significantly illustrated in another case:

A mother who had four live births and two stillbirths in twelve years lost all of her babies during their first year. She was so anxious that at least one child should live that she consulted a physician concerning the care of the last one. "Upon his advice," to quote the government report, "she gave up her twenty boarders immediately after the child's birth, and devoted all her time to

---

[1] U.S. Department of Labor: Children's Bureau. Infant Mortality Series, No. 3, pp. 81, 82, 83, 84.

it. Thinks she did not stop her hard work soon enough; says she has always worked too hard, keeping boarders in this country, and cutting wood and carrying it and water on her back in the old country. Also says the carrying of water and cases of beer in this country is a great strain on her." But the illuminating point in this case is that the father was furious because all the babies died. To show his disrespect for the wife who could only give birth to babies that died, he wore a red necktie to the funeral of the last. Yet this woman, the government agent reports, would follow and profit by any instruction that might be given her.

It is true that the cases reported from Johnstown, Pennsylvania, do not represent completely "Americanized" families. This lack does not prevent them, however, by their unceasing fertility from producing the Americans of to-morrow. Of the more immediate conditions surrounding child-birth, we are presented with this evidence, given by one woman concerning the birth of her last child:

On five o'clock on Wednesday evening she went to her sister's house to return a washboard, after finishing a day's washing. The baby was born while she was there. Her sister was too young to aid her in any way. She was not accustomed to a midwife, she confessed. She cut the cord herself, washed the new-born baby at her sister's house, walked home, cooked supper for her boarders, and went to bed by eight o'clock. The next day she got up and ironed. This tired her out, she said, so she stayed in bed for two whole days. She milked cows the day after the birth of the baby and sold the milk as well. Later in the week, when she became tired, she hired someone to do that portion of her work. This woman, we are further informed, kept cows, chickens, and lodgers, and earned additional money by doing laundry and charwork. At times her husband deserted her. His earnings amounted to $1.70 a day, while a fifteen-year-old son earned $1.10 in a coal mine.

One searches in vain for some picture of sacred motherhood, as depicted in popular plays and motion pictures, something more normal and encouraging. Then one comes to the bitter realization that these, in very truth, are the "normal" cases, not the exceptions. The exceptions are apt to indicate, instead, the close relationship of this irresponsible and chance parenthood to the great social problems of feeble-mindedness, crime and syphilis.

Nor is this type of motherhood confined to newly arrived immigrant mothers, as a government report from Akron, Ohio, sufficiently indicates. In this city, the government agents discovered that more than five hundred mothers were ignorant of the accepted principles of infant feeding, or, if familiar with them, did not practise them. "This ignorance or indifference was not confined to foreign-born mothers.... A native mother reported that she gave her two-weeks-old baby ice cream, and that before his sixth month, he was sitting at the table `eating everything."' This was in a town in which there were comparatively few cases of extreme poverty.

The degradation of motherhood, the damnation of the next generation before it is born, is exposed in all its catastrophic misery, in the reports of the National Consumers' League. In her report of living conditions among night-working mothers in thirty-nine textile mills in Rhode Island, based on exhaustive studies, Mrs. Florence Kelley describes the "normal" life of these women:

"When the worker, cruelly tired from ten hours' work, comes home in the early morning, she usually scrambles together breakfast for the family. Eating little or nothing herself, and that hastily, she tumbles into bed—not the immaculate bed in an airy bed-room with dark shades, but one still warm from its night occupants, in a stuffy little bed-room, darkened imperfectly if at all. After sleeping exhaustedly for an hour perhaps she bestirs herself to get the children off to school, or care for insistent little ones, too young to appreciate that mother is tired out and must sleep. Perhaps later in the forenoon, she again drops into a fitful sleep, or she may have to wait until after dinner. There is the midday meal to get, and, if her husband cannot come home, his dinner-pail to pack with a hot lunch to be sent or carried to him. If he is not at home, the lunch is rather a makeshift. The midday meal is scarcely over before supper must be thought of. This has to be eaten hurriedly before the family are ready, for the mother must be in the mill at work, by 6, 6:30 or 7 P.M.... Many women in their inadequate English, summed up their daily routine by, 'Oh, me all time tired. *Too much work, too much baby, too little sleep!*'"

"Only sixteen of the 166 married women were without children; thirty-two had three or more; twenty had children one year old or under. There were 160 children under school-age, below six years, and 246 of school age."

"A woman in ordinary circumstances," adds this impartial investigator, "with a husband and three children, if she does her own work, feels that her hands are full. How these mill-workers, many of them frail-looking, and many with confessedly poor health, can ever do two jobs is a mystery, when they are seen in their homes dragging about, pale, hollow-eyed and listless, often needlessly sharp and impatient with the children. These children are not only not mothered, never cherished, they are nagged and buffeted. The mothers are not superwomen, and like all human beings, they have a certain amount of strength and when that breaks, their nerves suffer."

We are presented with a vivid picture of one of these slave-mothers: a woman of thirty-eight who looks at least fifty with her worn, furrowed face. Asked why she had been working at night for the past two years, she pointed to a six-months old baby she was carrying, to the five small children swarming about her, and answered laconically, "Too much children!" She volunteered the information that there had been two more who had died. When asked why they had died, the poor mother shrugged her shoulders listlessly, and replied, "Don't know." In addition to bearing and rearing these children, her work would sap the vitality of any ordinary person. "She got home soon after four in the morning, cooked breakfast for the family and ate hastily herself. At 4.30 she was in bed, staying there until eight. But part of that time was disturbed for the children were noisy and the apartment was a tiny, dingy place in a basement. At eight she started the three oldest boys to school, and cleaned up the debris of breakfast and of supper the night before. At twelve she carried a hot lunch to her husband and had dinner ready for the three school children. In the afternoon, there were again dishes and cooking, and caring for three babies aged five, three years, and six months. At five, supper was ready for the family. The mother ate by herself and was off to work at 5:45."

Another of the night-working mothers was a frail looking Frenchwoman of twenty-seven years, with a husband and five children ranging from eight years to fourteen months. Three other children had died. When visited, she was doing a huge washing. She was forced into night work to meet the expenses of the family. She estimated that she succeeded in getting five hours' sleep during the day. "I take my baby to bed with me, but he cries, and my little four-year-old boy cries, too, and comes in to make me get up, so you can't call that a very good sleep."

The problem among unmarried women or those without family is not the same, this investigator points out. "They sleep longer by day than they normally would by night." We are also informed that pregnant women work at night in the mills, sometimes up to the very hour of delivery. "It's queer," exclaimed a woman supervisor of one of the Rhode Island mills, "but some women, both on the day and the night shift, will stick to their work right up to the last minute, and will use every means to deceive you about their condition. I go around and talk to them, but make little impression. We have had several narrow escapes.... A Polish mother with five children had worked in a mill by day or by night, ever since her marriage, stopping only to have her babies. One little girl had died several years ago, and the youngest child, says Mrs. Kelley, did not look promising. It had none of the charm of babyhood; its body and clothing were filthy; and its lower lip and chin covered with repulsive black sores."

It should be remembered that the Consumers' League, which publishes these reports on women in industry, is not advocating Birth Control education, but is aiming "to awaken responsibility for conditions under which goods are produced, and through investigation, education and legislation, to mobilize public opinion in behalf of enlightened standards for workers and honest products for all." Nevertheless, in Miss Agnes de Lima's report of conditions in Passaic, New Jersey, we find the same tale of penalized, prostrate motherhood, bearing the crushing burden of economic injustice and cruelty; the same blind but overpowering instincts of love and hunger driving young women into the factories to work, night in and night out, to support their procession of uncared for and undernourished babies. It is the married women with young children who work on the inferno-like shifts. They are driven to it

15

by the low wages of their husbands. They choose night work in order to be with their children in the daytime. They are afraid of the neglect and ill-treatment the children might receive at the hands of paid caretakers. Thus they condemn themselves to eighteen or twenty hours of daily toil. Surely no mother with three, four, five or six children can secure much rest by day.

"Take almost any house"—we read in the report of conditions in New Jersey—"knock at almost any door and you will find a weary, tousled woman, half-dressed, doing her housework, or trying to snatch an hour or two of sleep after her long night of work in the mill. ... The facts are there for any one to see; the hopeless and exhausted woman, her cluttered three or four rooms, the swarm of sickly and neglected children."

These women claimed that night work was unavoidable, as their husbands received so little pay. This in spite of all our vaunted "high wages." Only three women were found who went into the drudgery of night work without being obliged to do so. Two had no children, and their husbands' earnings were sufficient for their needs. One of these was saving for a trip to Europe, and chose the night shift because she found it less strenuous than the day. Only four of the hundred women reported upon were unmarried, and ninety-two of the married women had children. Of the four childless married women, one had lost two children, and another was recovering from a recent miscarriage. There were five widows. The average number of children was three in a family. Thirty-nine of the mothers had four or more. Three of them had six children, and six of them had seven children apiece. These women ranged between the ages of twenty-five and forty, and more than half the children were less than seven years of age. Most of them had babies of one, two and three years of age.

At the risk of repetition, we quote one of the typical cases reported by Miss De Lima with features practically identical with the individual cases reported from Rhode Island. It is of a mother who comes home from work at 5:30 every morning, falls on the bed from exhaustion, arises again at eight or nine o'clock to see that the older children are sent off to school. A son of five, like the rest of the children, is on a diet of coffee,—milk costs too much. After the children have left for school, the overworked mother again tries to sleep, though the small son bothers her a great deal. Besides, she must clean the house, wash, iron, mend, sew and prepare the midday meal. She tries to snatch a little sleep in the afternoon, but explains: "When you got big family, all time work. Night-time in mill drag so long, so long; day-time in home go so quick." By five, this mother must get the family's supper ready, and dress for the night's work, which begins at seven. The investigator further reports: "The next day was a holiday, and for a diversion, Mrs. N. thought she would go up to the cemetery: `I got some children up there,' she explained, `and same time I get some air. No, I don't go nowheres, just to the mill and then home.'"

Here again, as in all reports on women in industry, we find the prevalence of pregnant women working on night-shifts, often to the very day of their delivery. "Oh, yes, plenty women, big bellies, work in the night time," one of the toiling mothers volunteered. "Shame they go, but what can do?" The abuse was general. Many mothers confessed that owing to poverty they themselves worked up to the last week or even day before the birth of their children. Births were even reported in one of the mills during the night shift. A foreman told of permitting a night-working woman to leave at 6.30 one morning, and of the birth of her baby at 7.30. Several women told of leaving the day-shift because of pregnancy and of securing places on the night-shift where their condition was less conspicuous, and the bosses more tolerant. One mother defended her right to stay at work, says the report, claiming that as long as she could do her work, it was nobody's business. In a doorway sat a sickly and bloodless woman in an advanced stage of pregnancy. Her first baby had died of general debility. She had worked at night in the mill until the very day of its birth. This time the boss had told her she could stay if she wished, but reminded her of what had happened last time. So she had stopped work, as the baby was expected any day.

Again and again we read the same story, which varied only in detail: the mother in the three black rooms; the sagging porch overflowing with pale and sickly children; the over-worked mother of seven, still nursing her youngest, who is two or three months old. Worn and haggard, with a skeleton-like child pulling at her breast, the women tries to make the investigator understand. The grandmother helps to interpret. "She never sleeps," explains the old woman, "how can she with so many children?" She works up to the last moment before her baby comes, and returns to work as soon as they are four weeks old.

Another apartment in the same house; another of those night-working mothers, who had just stopped because she is pregnant. The boss had kindly given her permission to stay on, but she found the reaching on the heavy spinning machines too hard. Three children, ranging in age from five to twelve years, are all sickly and forlorn and must be cared for. There is a tubercular husband, who is unable to work steadily, and is able to bring in only $12 a week. Two of the babies had died, one because the mother had returned to work too soon after its birth and had lost her milk. She had fed him tea and bread, "so he died."

The most heartrending feature of it all—in these homes of the mothers who work at night—is the expression in the faces of the children; children of chance, dressed in rags, undernourished, underclothed, all predisposed to the ravages of chronic and epidemic disease.

The reports on infant mortality published under the direction of the Children's Bureau substantiate for the United States of America the findings of the Galton Laboratory for Great Britain, showing that an abnormally high rate of fertility is usually associated with poverty, filth, disease, feeblemindedness and a high infant mortality rate. It is a commonplace truism that a high birth-rate is accompanied by a high infant-mortality rate. No longer is it necessary to dissociate cause and effect, to try to determine whether the high birth rate is the cause of the high infant mortality rate. It is sufficient to know that they are organically correlated along with other anti-social factors detrimental to individual, national and racial welfare. The figures presented by Hibbs[2] likewise reveal a much higher infant mortality rate for the later born children of large families.

The statistics which show that the greatest number of children are born to parents whose earnings are the lowest,[3] that the direst poverty is associated with uncontrolled fecundity emphasize the character of the parenthood we are depending upon to create the race of the future.

A distinguished American opponent of Birth Control some years ago spoke of the "racial" value of this high infant mortality rate among the "unfit." He forgot, however, that the survival-rate of the children born of these overworked and fatigued mothers may nevertheless be large enough, aided and abetted by philanthropies and charities, to form the greater part of the population of to-morrow. As Dr. Karl Pearson has stated: "Degenerate stocks under present social conditions are not short-lived; they live to have more than the normal size of family."

Reports of charitable organizations; the famous "one hundred neediest cases" presented every year by the New York *Times* to arouse the sentimental generosity of its readers; statistics of public and private hospitals, charities and corrections; analyses of pauperism in town and country—all tell the same tale of uncontrolled and irresponsible fecundity. The facts, the figures, the appalling truth are there for all to read. It is only in the remedy proposed, the effective solution, that investigators and students of the problem disagree.

Confronted with the "startling and disgraceful" conditions of affairs indicated by the fact that a quarter of a million babies die every year in the United States before they are one year old, and that no less than 23,000 women die in childbirth, a large number of experts and enthusiasts have placed their hopes in maternity-benefit measures.

Such measures sharply illustrate the superficial and fragmentary manner in which the whole problem of motherhood is studied to-day. It seeks a *laisser faire* policy of parenthood or marriage, with an indiscriminating paternalism concerning maternity. It is as though the Government were to say: "Increase and multiply; we shall assume the responsibility of keeping your babies alive." Even granting that the administration of these measures might be made effective and effectual, which is more than doubtful, we see that they are based upon a complete ignorance or disregard of the most important fact in

---

[2] Henry H. Hibbs, Jr. Infant Mortality: Its Relation to Social and Industrial Con-ditions, p. 39. Russell Sage Foundation, New York, 1916.
[3] Cf. U. S. Department of Labor. Children's Bureau: Infant Mortality Series, No. 11. p. 36.

the situation—that of indiscriminate and irresponsible fecundity. They tacitly assume that all parenthood is desirable, that all children should be born, and that infant mortality can be controlled by external aid. In the great world-problem of creating the men and women of to-morrow, it is not merely a question of sustaining the lives of all children, irrespective of their hereditary and physical qualities, to the point where they, in turn, may reproduce their kind. Advocates of Birth Control offer and accept no such superficial solution. This philosophy is based upon a clearer vision and a more profound comprehension of human life. Of immediate relief for the crushed and enslaved motherhood of the world through State aid, no better criticism has been made than that of Havelock Ellis:

"To the theoretical philanthropist, eager to reform the world on paper, nothing seems simpler than to cure the present evils of child-rearing by setting up State nurseries which are at once to relieve mothers of everything connected with the men of the future beyond the pleasure—if such it happens to be—of conceiving them, and the trouble of bearing them, and at the same time to rear them up independently of the home, in a wholesome, economical and scientific manner. Nothing seems simpler, but from the fundamental psychological point of view nothing is falser.... A State which admits that the individuals composing it are incompetent to perform their most sacred and intimate functions, and takes it upon itself to perform them itself instead, attempts a task that would be undesirable, even if it were possible of achievement."[4] It may be replied that maternity benefit measures aim merely to aid mothers more adequately to fulfil their biological and social functions. But from the point of view of Birth Control, that will never be possible until the crushing exigencies of overcrowding are removed—overcrowding of pregnancies as well as of homes. As long as the mother remains the passive victim of blind instinct, instead of the conscious, responsible instrument of the life-force, controlling and directing its expression, there can be no solution to the intricate and complex problems that confront the whole world to-day. This is, of course, impossible as long as women are driven into the factories, on night as well as day shifts, as long as children and girls and young women are driven into industries to labor that is physically deteriorating as a preparation for the supreme function of maternity.

The philosophy of Birth Control insists that motherhood, no less than any other human function, must undergo scientific study, must be voluntarily directed and controlled with intelligence and foresight. As long as we countenance what H. G. Wells has well termed "the monstrous absurdity of women discharging their supreme social function, bearing and rearing children, in their spare time, as it were, while they 'earn their living' by contributing some half-mechanical element to some trivial industrial product" any attempt to furnish "maternal education" is bound to fall on stony ground.

---

[4] Havelock Ellis, Sex in Relation to Society, p. 31.

Children brought into the world as the chance consequences of the blind play of uncontrolled instinct, become likewise the helpless victims of their environment. It is because children are cheaply conceived that the infant mortality rate is high. But the greatest evil, perhaps the greatest crime, of our so-called civilization of to-day, is not to be gauged by the infant-mortality rate. In truth, unfortunate babies who depart during their first twelve months are more fortunate in many respects than those who survive to undergo punishment for their parents' cruel ignorance and complacent fecundity. If motherhood is wasted under the present regime of "glorious fertility," childhood is not merely wasted, but actually destroyed. Let us look at this matter from the point of view of the children who survive.

CHAPTER III: "Children Troop Down From Heaven...."

Failure of emotional, sentimental and so-called idealistic efforts, based on hysterical enthusiasm, to improve social conditions, is nowhere better exemplified than in the undervaluation of child-life. A few years ago, the scandal of children under fourteen working in cotton mills was exposed. There was muckraking and agitation. A wave of moral indignation swept over America. There arose a loud cry for immediate action. Then, having more or less successfully settled this particular matter, the American people heaved a sigh of relief, settled back, and complacently congratulated itself that the problem of child labor had been settled once and for all.

Conditions are worse to-day than before. Not only is there child labor in practically every State in the Union, but we are now forced to realize the evils that result from child labor, of child laborers now grown into manhood and womanhood. But we wish here to point out a neglected aspect of this problem. Child labor shows us how cheaply we value childhood. And moreover, it shows us that cheap childhood is the inevitable result of chance parenthood. Child labor is organically bound up with the problem of uncontrolled breeding and the large family.

The selective draft of 1917—which was designed to choose for military service only those fulfilling definite requirements of physical and mental fitness—showed some of the results of child labor. It established the fact that the majority of American children never got beyond the sixth grade, because they were forced to leave school at that time. Our over-advertised compulsory education does not compel—and does not educate. The selective-draft, it is our duty to emphasize this fact, revealed that 38 per cent. of the young men (more than a million) were rejected because of physical ill-health and defects. And 25 per cent. were illiterate.

These young men were the children of yesterday. Authorities tell us that 75 per cent. of the school-children are defective. This means that no less than fifteen million schoolchildren, out of 22,000,000 in the United States, are physically or mentally below par.

This is the soil in which all sorts of serious evils strike root. It is a truism that children are the chief asset of a nation. Yet while the United States government allotted 92.8 per cent. of its appropriations for 1920 toward war expenses, three per cent. to public works, 3.2 per cent. to "primary governmental functions," no more than one per cent. is appropriated to education, research and development. Of this one per cent., only a small proportion is devoted to public health. The conservation of childhood is a minor consideration. While three cents is spent for the more or less doubtful protection of women and children, fifty cents is given to the Bureau of Animal Industry, for the protection of domestic animals. In 1919, the State of

Kansas appropriated $25,000 to protect the health of pigs, and $4,000 to protect the health of children. In four years our Federal Government appropriated—roughly speaking—$81,000,000 for the improvement of rivers; $13,000,000 for forest conservation; $8,000,000 for the experimental plant industry; $7,000,000 for the experimental animal industry; $4,000,000 to combat the foot and mouth disease; and less than half a million for the protection of child life.

Competent authorities tell us that no less than 75 per cent. of American children leave school between the ages of fourteen and sixteen to go to work. This number is increasing. According to the recently published report on "The Administration of the First Child Labor Law," in five states in which it was necessary for the Children's Bureau to handle directly the working certificates of children, one-fifth of the 25,000 children who applied for certificates left school when they were in the fourth grade; nearly a tenth of them had never attended school at all or had not gone beyond the first grade; and only one-twenty-fifth had gone as far as the eighth grade. But their educational equipment was even more limited than the grade they attended would indicate. Of the children applying to go to work 1,803 had not advanced further than the first grade even when they had gone to school at all; 3,379 could not even sign their own names legibly, and nearly 2,000 of them could not write at all. The report brings automatically into view the vicious circle of child-labor, illiteracy, bodily and mental defect, poverty and delinquency. And like all reports on child labor, the large family and reckless breeding looms large in the background as one of the chief factors in the problem.

Despite all our boasting of the American public school, of the equal opportunity afforded to every child in America, we have the shortest school-term, and the shortest school-day of any of the civilized countries. In the United States of America, there are 106 illiterates to every thousand people. In England there are 58 per thousand, Sweden and Norway have one per thousand.

The United States is the most illiterate country in the world—that is, of the so-called civilized countries. Of the 5,000,000 illiterates in the United States, 58 per cent. are white and 28 per cent. native whites. Illiteracy not only is the index of inequality of opportunity. It speaks as well a lack of consideration for the children. It means either that children have been forced out of school to go to work, or that they are mentally and physically defective.[5]

One is tempted to ask why a society, which has failed so lamentably to protect the already existing child life upon which its very perpetuation depends, takes upon itself the reckless encouragement of indiscriminate procreation. The United States Government has recently inaugurated a policy of restricting immigration from foreign countries. Until it is able to protect

---

[5] I am indebted to the National Child Labor Committee for these statistics, as well as for many of the facts that follow.

childhood from criminal exploitation, until it has made possible a reasonable hope of life, liberty and growth for American children, it should likewise recognize the wisdom of voluntary restriction in the production of children.

Reports on child labor published by the National Child Labor Committee only incidentally reveal the correlation of this evil with that of large families. Yet this is evident throughout. The investigators are more bent upon regarding child labor as a cause of illiteracy.

But it is no less a consequence of irresponsibility in breeding. A sinister aspect of this is revealed by Theresa Wolfson's study of child-labor in the beet-fields of Michigan.[6] As one weeder put it: "Poor man make no money, make plenty children—plenty children good for sugar-beet business." Further illuminating details are given by Miss Wolfson:

"Why did they come to the beet-fields? Most frequently families with large numbers of children said that they felt that the city was no place to raise children—things too expensive and children ran wild—in the country all the children could work." Living conditions are abominable and unspeakably wretched. An old woodshed, a long-abandoned barn, and occasionally a tottering, ramshackle farmer's house are the common types. "One family of eleven, the youngest child two years, the oldest sixteen years, lived in an old country store which had but one window; the wind and rain came through the holes in the walls, the ceiling was very low and the smoke from the stove filled the room. Here the family ate, slept, cooked and washed."

"In Tuscola County a family of six was found living in a one-room shack with no windows. Light and ventilation was secured through the open doors. Little Charles, eight years of age, was left at home to take care of Dan, Annie and Pete, whose ages were five years, four years, and three months, respectively. In addition, he cooked the noonday meal and brought it to his parents in the field. The filth and choking odors of the shack made it almost unbearable, yet the baby was sleeping in a heap of rags piled up in a corner."

Social philosophers of a certain school advocate the return to the land—it is only in the overcrowded city, they claim, that the evils resulting from the large family are possible. There is, according to this philosophy, no overcrowding, no over-population in the country, where in the open air and sunlight every child has an opportunity for health and growth. This idyllic conception of American country life does not correspond with the picture presented by this investigator, who points out:

"To promote the physical and mental development of the child, we forbid his employment in factories, shops and stores. On the other hand, we are prone to believe that the right kind of farm-work is healthful and the best thing for children. But for a child to crawl along the ground, weeding beets in the hot sun for fourteen hours a day—the average workday—is far from being the best thing. The law of compensation is bound to work in some way, and

---

[6] "People Who Go to Beets" Pamphlet No. 299, National Child Labor Committee.

the immediate result of this agricultural work is interference with school attendance."

How closely related this form of child-slavery is to the over-large family, is definitely illustrated: "In the one hundred and thirty-three families visited, there were six hundred children. A conversation held with a 'Rooshian-German' woman is indicative of the size of most of the families:"

"How many children have you?" inquired the investigator.

"Eight—Julius, und Rose, und Martha, dey is mine; Gottlieb und Philip, und Frieda, dey is my husband's;—und Otto und Charlie—dey are ours."

Families with ten and twelve children were frequently found, while those of six and eight children are the general rule. The advantage of a large family in the beet fields is that it does the most work. In the one hundred thirty-three families interviewed, there were one hundred eighty-six children under the age of six years, ranging from eight weeks up; thirty-six children between the ages of six and eight, approximately twenty-five of whom had never been to school, and eleven over sixteen years of age who had never been to school. One ten-year-old boy had never been to school because he was a mental defective; one child of nine was practically blinded by cataracts. This child was found groping his way down the beet-rows pulling out weeds and feeling for the beet-plants—in the glare of the sun he had lost all sense of light and dark. Of the three hundred and forty children who were not going or had never gone to school, only four had reached the point of graduation, and only one had gone to high school. These large families migrated to the beet-fields in early spring. Seventy-two per cent. of them are retarded. When we realize that feeble-mindedness is arrested development and retardation, we see that these "beet children" are artificially retarded in their growth, and that the tendency is to reduce their intelligence to the level of the congenital imbecile.

Nor must it be concluded that these large "beet" families are always the "ignorant foreigner" so despised by our respectable press. The following case throws some light on this matter, reported in the same pamphlet: "An American family, considered a prize by the agent because of the fact that there were nine children, turned out to be a `flunk.' They could not work in the beet-fields, they ran up a bill at the country-store, and one day the father and the eldest son, a boy of nineteen, were seen running through the railroad station to catch an out-going train. The grocer thought they were `jumping' their bill. He telephoned ahead to the sheriff of the next town. They were taken off the train by the sheriff and given the option of going back to the farm or staying in jail. They preferred to stay in jail, and remained there for two weeks. Meanwhile, the mother and her eight children, ranging in ages form seventeen years to nine months, had to manage the best way they could. At the end of two weeks, father and son were set free.... During all of this period the farmers of the community sent in provisions to keep the wife and children from starving." Does this case not sum up in a nutshell the typical

American intelligence confronted with the problem of the too-large family—industrial slavery tempered with sentimentality!

Let us turn to a young, possibly a more progressive state. Consider the case of "California, the Golden" as it is named by Emma Duke, in her study of child-labor in the Imperial Valley, "as fertile as the Valley of the Nile."[7] Here, cotton is king, and rich ranchers, absentee landlords and others exploit it. Less than ten years ago ranchers would bring in hordes of laboring families, but refuse to assume any responsibility in housing them, merely permitting them to sleep on the grounds of the ranch. Conditions have been somewhat improved, but, sometimes, we read, "a one roomed straw house with an area of fifteen by twenty feet will serve as a home for an entire family, which not only cooks but sleeps in the same room." Here, as in Michigan among the beets, children are "thick as bees." All kinds of children pick, Miss Duke reports, "even those as young as three years! Five-year-old children pick steadily all day.... Many white American children are among them—pure American stock, who have gradually moved from the Carolinas, Tennessee, and other southern states to Arkansas, Texas, Oklahoma, Arizona, and on into the Imperial Valley." Some of these children, it seems, wanted to attend school, but their fathers did not want to work; so the children were forced to become bread-winners. One man whose children were working with him in the fields said, "Please, lady, don't send them to school; let them pick a while longer. I ain't got my new auto paid for yet." The native white American mother of children working in the fields proudly remarked: "No; they ain't never been to school, nor me nor their poppy, nor their granddads and grandmoms. We've always been pickers!"—and she spat her tobacco over the field in expert fashion.

"In the Valley one hears from townspeople," writes the investigator, "that pickers make ten dollars a day, working the whole family. With that qualification, the statement is ambiguous. One Mexican in the Imperial Valley was the father of thirty-three children—'about thirteen or fourteen living,' he said. If they all worked at cotton-picking, they would doubtless altogether make more than ten dollars a day."

One of the child laborers revealed the economic advantage—to the parents—in numerous progeny: "Us kids most always drag from forty to fifty pounds of cotton before we take it to be weighed. Three of us pick. I'm twelve years old and my bag is twelve feet long. I can drag nearly a hundred pounds. My sister is ten years old, and her bag is eight feet long. My little brother is seven and his bag is five feet long."

---

[7] California the Golden, by Emma Duke. Reprinted from The American Child, Vol. II, No. 3. November 1920.

Evidence abounds in the publications of the National Child Labor Committee of this type of fecund parenthood.[8] It is not merely a question of the large family versus the small family. Even comparatively small families among migratory workers of this sort have been large families. The high infant mortality rate has carried off the weaker children. Those who survive are merely those who have been strong enough to survive the most unfavorable living conditions. No; it is a situation not unique, nor even unusual in human history, of greed and stupidity and cupidity encouraging the procreative instinct toward the manufacture of slaves. We hear these days of the selfishness and the degradation of healthy and well-educated women who refuse motherhood; but we hear little of the more sinister selfishness of men and women who bring babies into the world to become child-slaves of the kind described in these reports of child labor.

The history of child labor in the English factories in the nineteenth century throws a suggestive light on this situation. These child-workers were really called into being by the industrial situation. The population grew, as Dean Inge has described it, like crops in a newly irrigated desert. During the nineteenth century, the numbers were nearly quadrupled. "Let those who think that the population of a country can be increased at will, consider whether it is likely that any physical, moral, or psychological change came over the nation co-incidentally with the inventions of the spinning jenny and the steam engine. It is too obvious for dispute that it was the possession of capital wanting employment, and of natural advantages for using it, that called those multitudes of human beings into existence, to eat the food which they paid for by their labor."[9]

But when child labor in the factories became such a scandal and such a disgrace that child-labor was finally forbidden by laws that possessed the advantage over our own that they were enforced, the proletariat ceased to supply children. Almost by magic the birth rate among the workers declined. Since children were no longer of economic value to the factories, they were evidently a drug in the home. This movement, it should not be forgotten however, was coincident with the agitation and education in Birth Control stimulated by the Besant-Bradlaugh trial.

Large families among migratory agricultural laborers in our own country are likewise brought into existence in response to an industrial demand. The enforcement of the child labor laws and the extension of their restrictions are therefore an urgent necessity, not so much, as some of our child-labor authorities believe, to enable these children to go to school, as to prevent the recruiting of our next generation from the least intelligent and most unskilled

---

[8] Cf. Child Welfare in Oklahoma; Child Welfare in Alabama; Child Welfare in North Carolina; Child Welfare in Kentucky; Child Welfare in Tennessee. Also, Children in Agriculture, by Ruth McIntire, and other studies.
[9] W. R. Inge: Outspoken Essays: p. 92.

classes in the community. As long as we officially encourage and countenance the production of large families, the evils of child labor will confront us. On the other hand, the prohibition of child labor may help, as in the case of English factories, in the decline of the birth rate.

Uncontrolled breeding and child labor go hand in hand. And to-day when we are confronted with the evils of the latter, in the form of widespread illiteracy and defect, we should seek causes more deeply rooted than the enslavement of children. The cost to society is incalculable, as the National Child Labor Committee points out. "It is not only through the lowered power, the stunting and the moral degeneration of its individual members, but in actual expense, through the necessary provision for the human junk, created by premature employment, in poor-houses, hospitals, police and courts, jails and by charitable organizations."

To-day we are paying for the folly of the over-production—and its consequences in permanent injury to plastic childhood—of yesterday. To-morrow, we shall be forced to pay for our ruthless disregard of our surplus children of to-day. The child-laborer of one or two decades ago has become the shifting laborer of to-day, stunted, underfed, illiterate, unskilled, unorganized and unorganizable. "He is the last person to be hired and the first to be fired." Boys and girls under fourteen years of age are no longer permitted to work in factories, mills, canneries and establishments whose products are to be shipped out of the particular state, and children under sixteen can no longer work in mines and quarries. But this affects only one quarter of our army of child labor—work in local industries, stores, and farms, homework in dark and unsanitary tenements is still permitted. Children work in "homes" on artificial flowers, finishing shoddy garments, sewing their very life's blood and that of the race into tawdry clothes and gewgaws that are the most unanswerable comments upon our vaunted "civilization." And to-day, we must not forget, the child-laborer of yesterday is becoming the father or the mother of the child-laborer of to-morrow.

"Any nation that works its women is damned," once wrote Woods Hutchinson. The nation that works its children, one is tempted to add, is committing suicide. Loud-mouthed defenders of American democracy pay no attention to the strange fact that, although "the average education among all American adults is only the sixth grade," every one of these adults has an equal power at the polls. The American nation, with all its worship of efficiency and thrift, complacently forgets that "every child defective in body, education or character is a charge upon the community," as Herbert Hoover declared in an address before the American Child Hygiene Association (October, 1920): "The nation as a whole," he added, "has the obligation of such measures toward its children... as will yield to them an equal opportunity at their start in life. If we could grapple with the whole child situation for one generation, our public health, our economic efficiency, the moral character, sanity and stability of our people would advance three generations in one."

27

The great irrefutable fact that is ignored or neglected is that the American nation officially places a low value upon the lives of its children. The brutal truth is that *children are cheap*. When over-production in this field is curtailed by voluntary restriction, when the birth rate among the working classes takes a sharp decline, the value of children will rise. Then only will the infant mortality rate decline, and child labor vanish.

Investigations of child labor emphasize its evils by pointing out that these children are kept out of school, and that they miss the advantages of American public school education. They express the current confidence in compulsory education and the magical benefits to be derived from the public school. But we need to qualify our faith in education, and particularly our faith in the American public school. Educators are just beginning to wake up to the dangers inherent in the attempt to teach the brightest child and the mentally defective child at the same time. They are beginning to test the possibilities of a "vertical" classification as well as a "horizontal" one. That is, each class must be divided into what are termed Gifted, Bright, Average, Dull, Normal, and Defective. In the past the helter-skelter crowding and over-crowding together of all classes of children of approximately the same age, produced only a dull leveling to mediocrity.[10]

An investigation of forty schools in New York City, typical of hundreds of others, reveals deplorable conditions of overcrowding and lack of sanitation.[11] The worst conditions are to be found in locations the most densely populated. Thus of Public School No. 51, located almost in the center of the notorious "Hell's Kitchen" section, we read: "The play space which is provided is a mockery of the worst kind. The basement play-room is dark, damp, poorly lighted, poorly ventilated, foul smelling, unclean, and wholly unfit for children for purposes of play. The drainpipes from the roof have decayed to such a degree that in some instances as little as a quarter of the pipe remains. On rainy days, water enters the classrooms, hallways, corridors, and is thrown against windows because the pipes have rotted away. The narrow stairways and halls are similar to those of jails and dungeons of a century ago. The classrooms are poorly lighted, inadequately equipped, and in some cases so small that the desks of pupils and teachers occupy almost all of the floor-space."

Another school, located a short distance from Fifth Avenue, the "wealthiest street in the world," is described as an "old shell of a structure, erected decades ago as a modern school building. Nearly two thousand children are crowded into class-rooms having a total seating capacity of scarcely one thousand. Narrow doorways, intricate hallways and antiquated stairways, dark and precipitous, keep ever alive the danger of disaster from

---

[10] Cf. Tredgold: Inheritance and Educability. Eugenics Review, Vol. Xiii, No. I, pp. 839 et seq.

[11] Cf. New York Times, June 4, 1921.

fire or panic. Only the eternal vigilance of exceptional supervision has served to lessen the fear of such a catastrophe. Artificial light is necessary, even on the brightest days, in many of the class-rooms. In most of the classrooms, it is always necessary when the sky is slightly overcast." There is no ventilating system.

In the crowded East Side section conditions are reported to be no better. The Public Education Association's report on Public School No. 130 points out that the site at the corner of Hester and Baxter Streets was purchased by the city years ago as a school site, but that there has been so much "tweedledeeing and tweedleduming" that the new building which is to replace the old, has not even yet been planned! Meanwhile, year after year, thousands of children are compelled to study daily in dark and dingy class-rooms. "Artificial light is continually necessary," declares the report. "The ventilation is extremely poor. The fire hazard is naturally great. There are no rest-rooms whatever for the teachers." Other schools in the neighborhood reveal conditions even worse. In two of them, for example; "In accordance with the requirements of the syllabus in hygiene in the schools, the vision of the children is regularly tested. In a recent test of this character, it was found in Public School 108, the rate of defective vision in the various grades ranged from 50 to 64 per cent.! In Public School 106, the rate ranged from 43 to 94 per cent.!"

The conditions, we are assured, are no exceptions to the rule of public schools in New York, where the fatal effects of overcrowding in education may be observed in their most sinister but significant aspects.

The forgotten fact in this case is that efforts for universal and compulsory education cannot keep pace with the overproduction of children. Even at the best, leaving out of consideration the public school system as the inevitable prey and plundering-ground of the cheap politician and job-hunter, present methods of wholesale and syndicated "education" are not suited to compete with the unceasing, unthinking, untiring procreative powers of our swarming, spawning populations.

Into such schools as described in the recent reports of the Public Education Association, no intelligent parent would dare send his child. They are not merely fire-traps and culture-grounds of infection, but of moral and intellectual contamination as well. More and more are public schools in America becoming institutions for subjecting children to a narrow and reactionary orthodoxy, aiming to crush out all signs of individuality, and to turn out boys and girls compressed into a standardized pattern, with ready-made ideas on politics, religion, morality, and economics. True education cannot grow out of such compulsory herding of children in filthy fire-traps.

Character, ability, and reasoning power are not to be developed in this fashion. Indeed, it is to be doubted whether even a completely successful educational system could offset the evils of indiscriminate breeding and compensate for the misfortune of being a superfluous child. In recognizing the

29

great need of education, we have failed to recognize the greater need of inborn health and character. "If it were necessary to choose between the task of getting children educated and getting them well born and healthy," writes Havelock Ellis, "it would be better to abandon education. There have been many great peoples who never dreamed of national systems of education; there have been no great peoples without the art of producing healthy and vigorous children. The matter becomes of peculiar importance in great industrial states, like England, the United States and Germany, because in such states, a tacit conspiracy tends to grow up to subordinate national ends to individual ends, and practically to work for the deterioration of the race."[12]

Much less can education solve the great problem of child labor. Rather, under the conditions prevailing in modern society, child labor and the failure of the public schools to educate are both indices of a more deeply rooted evil. Both bespeak *The Undervaluation of the Child*. This undervaluation, this cheapening of child life, is to speak crudely but frankly the direct result of overproduction. "Restriction of output" is an immediate necessity if we wish to regain control of the real values, so that unimpeded, unhindered, and without danger of inner corruption, humanity may protect its own health and powers.

---

[12] "Studies in the Psychology of Sex," Vol. VI. p. 20.

CHAPTER IV: The Fertility of the Feeble-Minded

What vesture have you woven for my year?
O Man and Woman who have fashioned it
Together, is it fine and clean and strong,
Made in such reverence of holy joy,
Of such unsullied substance, that your hearts
Leap with glad awe to see it clothing me,
The glory of whose nakedness you know?

"The Song of the Unborn"
Amelia Josephine Burr

There is but one practical and feasible program in handling the great problem of the feeble-minded. That is, as the best authorities are agreed, to prevent the birth of those who would transmit imbecility to their descendants. Feeble-mindedness as investigations and statistics from every country indicate, is invariably associated with an abnormally high rate of fertility. Modern conditions of civilization, as we are continually being reminded, furnish the most favorable breeding-ground for the mental defective, the moron, the imbecile. "We protect the members of a weak strain," says Davenport, "up to the period of reproduction, and then let them free upon the community, and encourage them to leave a large progeny of 'feeble-minded': which in turn, protected from mortality and carefully nurtured up to the reproductive period, are again set free to reproduce, and so the stupid work goes on of preserving and increasing our socially unfit strains."

The philosophy of Birth Control points out that as long as civilized communities encourage unrestrained fecundity in the "normal" members of the population—always of course under the cloak of decency and morality— and penalize every attempt to introduce the principle of discrimination and responsibility in parenthood, they will be faced with the ever-increasing problem of feeble-mindedness, that fertile parent of degeneracy, crime, and pauperism. Small as the percentage of the imbecile and half-witted may seem in comparison with the normal members of the community, it should always be remembered that feeble-mindedness is not an unrelated expression of modern civilization. Its roots strike deep into the social fabric. Modern studies indicate that insanity, epilepsy, criminality, prostitution, pauperism, and mental defect, are all organically bound up together and that the least intelligent and the thoroughly degenerate classes in every community are the most prolific. Feeble-mindedness in one generation becomes pauperism or insanity in the next. There is every indication that feeble-mindedness in its protean forms is on the increase, that it has leaped the barriers, and that there is truly, as some of the scientific eugenists have pointed out, a feeble-minded peril to future generations—unless the feeble-minded are prevented from reproducing their kind. To meet this emergency is the immediate and peremptory duty of every State and of all communities.

The curious situation has come about that while our statesmen are busy upon their propaganda of "repopulation," and are encouraging the production of large families, they are ignoring the exigent problem of the elimination of the feeble-minded. In this, however, the politicians are at one with the traditions of a civilization which, with its charities and philanthropies, has propped up the defective and degenerate and relieved them of the burdens borne by the healthy sections of the community, thus enabling them more easily and more numerously to propagate their kind. "With the very highest motives," declares Dr. Walter E. Fernald, "modern philanthropic efforts often tend to foster and increase the growth of defect in the community.... The only feeble-minded persons who now receive any official consideration are those who have already become dependent or delinquent, many of whom have already become parents. We lock the barn-door after the horse is stolen. We now have state commissions for controlling the gipsy-moth and the boll weevil, the foot-and-mouth disease, and for protecting the shell-fish and wild game, but we have no commission which even attempts to modify or to control the vast moral and economic forces represented by the feeble-minded persons at large in the community."

How the feeble-minded and their always numerous progeny run the gamut of police, alms-houses, courts, penal institutions, "charities and corrections," tramp shelters, lying-in hospitals, and relief afforded by privately endowed religious and social agencies, is shown in any number of reports and studies of family histories. We find cases of feeble-mindedness and mental defect in the reports on infant mortality referred to in a previous chapter, as well as in other reports published by the United States government. Here is a typical case showing the astonishing ability to "increase and multiply," organically bound up with delinquency and defect of various types:

"The parents of a feeble-minded girl, twenty years of age, who was committed to the Kansas State Industrial Farm on a vagrancy charge, lived in a thickly populated Negro district which was reported by the police to be the headquarters for the criminal element of the surrounding State.... The mother married at fourteen, and her first child was born at fifteen. In rapid succession she gave birth to sixteen live-born children and had one miscarriage. The first child, a girl, married but separated from her husband.... The fourth, fifth and sixth, all girls, died in infancy or early childhood. The seventh, a girl, remarried after the death of her husband, from whom she had been separated. The eighth, a boy who early in life began to exhibit criminal tendencies, was in prison for highway robbery and burglary. The ninth, a girl, normal mentally, was in quarantine at the Kansas State Industrial Farm at the time this study was made; she had lived with a man as his common-law wife, and had also been arrested several times for soliciting. The tenth, a boy, was involved in several delinquencies when young and was sent to the detention-

32

house but did not remain there long. The eleventh, a boy... at the age of seventeen was sentenced to the penitentiary for twenty years on a charge of first-degree robbery; after serving a portion of his time, he was paroled, and later was shot and killed in a fight. The twelfth, a boy, was at fifteen years of age implicated in a murder and sent to the industrial school, but escaped from there on a bicycle which he had stolen; at eighteen, he was shot and killed by a woman. The thirteenth child, feeble-minded, is the girl of the study. The fourteenth, a boy was considered by police to be the best member of the family; his mother reported him to be much slower mentally than his sister just mentioned; he had been arrested several times. Once, he was held in the detention-home and once sent to the State Industrial school; at other times, he was placed on probation. The fifteenth, a girl sixteen years old, has for a long time had a bad reputation. Subsequent to the commitment of her sister to the Kansas State Industrial Farm, she was arrested on a charge of vagrancy, found to be syphilitic, and quarantined in a state other than Kansas. At the time of her arrest, she stated that prostitution was her occupation. The last child was a boy of thirteen years whose history was not secured...."[13]

The notorious fecundity of feeble-minded women is emphasized in studies and investigations of the problem, coming from all countries. "The feeble-minded woman is twice as prolific as the normal one." Sir James Crichton-Browne speaks of the great numbers of feeble-minded girls, wholly unfit to become mothers, who return to the work-house year after year to bear children, "many of whom happily die, but some of whom survive to recruit our idiot establishments and to repeat their mothers' performances." Tredgold points out that the number of children born to the feeble-minded is abnormally high. Feeble-minded women "constitute a permanent menace to the race and one which becomes serious at a time when the decline of the birth-rate is... unmistakable." Dr. Tredgold points out that "the average number of children born in a family is four," whereas in these degenerate families, we find an average of 7.3 to each. Out of this total only a little more than *one-third*—456 out of a total of 1,269 children—can be considered profitable members of the community, and that, be it remembered, at the parents' valuation.

Another significant point is the number of mentally defective children who survive. "Out of the total number of 526 mentally affected persons in the 150 families, there are 245 in the present generation—an unusually large survival."[14]

---

[13] United States Public Health Service: Psychiatric Studies of Delinquents. Reprint No. 598: pp. 64-65.
[14] The Problem of the Feeble-Minded: An Abstract of the Report of the Royal Commission on the Cure and Control of the Feeble-Minded, London: P. S. King & Son.

Speaking for Bradford, England, Dr. Helen U. Campbell touches another significant and interesting point usually neglected by the advocates of mothers' pensions, milk-stations, and maternity-education programs.

"We are also confronted with the problem of the actually mentally deficient, of the more or less feeble-minded, and the deranged, epileptic... or otherwise mentally abnormal mother," writes this authority. "The `bad mothering' of these cases is quite unimprovable at an infant welfare center, and a very definite if not relatively very large percentage of our infants are suffering severely as a result of dependence upon such `mothering.'"[15]

Thus we are brought face to face with another problem of infant mortality. Are we to check the infant mortality rate among the feeble-minded and aid the unfortunate offspring to grow up, a menace to the civilized community even when not actually certifiable as mentally defective or not obviously imbecile?

Other figures and studies indicate the close relationship between feeble-mindedness and the spread of venereal scourges. We are informed that in Michigan, 75 per cent. of the prostitute class is infected with some form of venereal disease, and that 75 per cent. of the infected are mentally defective,—morons, imbeciles, or "border-line" cases most dangerous to the community at large. At least 25 per cent. of the inmates of our prisons, according to Dr. Fernald, are mentally defective and belong either to the feeble-minded or to the defective-delinquent class. Nearly 50 per cent. of the girls sent to reformatories are mental defectives. To-day, society treats feeble-minded or "defective delinquent" men or women as "criminals," sentences them to prison or reformatory for a "term," and then releases them at the expiration of their sentences. They are usually at liberty just long enough to reproduce their kind, and then they return again and again to prison. The truth of this statement is evident from the extremely large proportion in institutions of neglected and dependent children, who are the feeble-minded offspring of such feeble-minded parents.

Confronted with these shocking truths about the menace of feeble-mindedness to the race, a menace acute because of the unceasing and unrestrained fertility of such defectives, we are apt to become the victims of a "wild panic for instant action." There is no occasion for hysterical, ill-considered action, specialists tell us. They direct our attention to another phase of the problem, that of the so-called "good feeble-minded." We are informed that imbecility, in itself, is not synonymous with badness. If it is fostered in a "suitable environment," it may express itself in terms of good citizenship and useful occupation. It may thus be transmuted into a docile, tractable, and peaceable element of the community. The moron and the feeble-minded, thus protected, so we are assured, may even marry some brighter member of the community, and thus lessen the chances of procreating

---

[15] Cf. Feeble-Minded in Ontario: Fourteenth Report for the year ending October 31st, 1919.

another generation of imbeciles. We read further that some of our doctors believe that "in our social scale, there is a place for the good feeble-minded."

In such a reckless and thoughtless differentiation between the "bad" and the "good" feeble-minded, we find new evidence of the conventional middle-class bias that also finds expression among some of the eugenists. We do not object to feeble-mindedness simply because it leads to immorality and criminality; nor can we approve of it when it expresses itself in docility, submissiveness and obedience. We object because both are burdens and dangers to the intelligence of the community. As a matter of fact, there is sufficient evidence to lead us to believe that the so-called "borderline cases" are a greater menace than the out-and-out "defective delinquents" who can be supervised, controlled and prevented from procreating their kind. The advent of the Binet-Simon and similar psychological tests indicates that the mental defective who is glib and plausible, bright looking and attractive, but with a mental vision of seven, eight or nine years, may not merely lower the whole level of intelligence in a school or in a society, but may be encouraged by church and state to increase and multiply until he dominates and gives the prevailing "color"—culturally speaking—to an entire community.

The presence in the public schools of the mentally defective children of men and women who should never have been parents is a problem that is becoming more and more difficult, and is one of the chief reasons for lower educational standards. As one of the greatest living authorities on the subject, Dr. A. Tredgold, has pointed out,[16] this has created a destructive conflict of purpose. "In the case of children with a low intellectual capacity, much of the education at present provided is for all practical purposes a complete waste of time, money and patience.... On the other hand, for children of high intellectual capacity, our present system does not go far enough. I believe that much innate potentiality remains undeveloped, even amongst the working classes, owing to the absence of opportunity for higher education, to the disadvantage of the nation. In consequence of these fundamental differences, the catchword `equality of opportunity' is meaningless and mere claptrap in the absence of any equality to respond to such opportunity. What is wanted is not equality of opportunity, but education adapted to individual potentiality; and if the time and money now spent in the fruitless attempt to make silk-purses out of sows' ears, were devoted to the higher education of children of good natural capacity, it would contribute enormously to national efficiency."

In a much more complex manner than has been recognized even by students of this problem, the destiny and the progress of civilization and of human expression has been hindered and held back by this burden of the imbecile and the moron. While we may admire the patience and the deep human sympathy with which the great specialists in feeble-mindedness have expressed the hope of drying up the sources of this evil or of rendering it

---

[16] Eugenics Review, Vol. XIII, p. 339 et seq.

harmless, we should not permit sympathy or sentimentality to blind us to the fact that health and vitality and human growth likewise need cultivation. "A *laisser faire* policy," writes one investigator, "simply allows the social sore to spread. And a quasi *laisser faire* policy wherein we allow the defective to commit crime and then interfere and imprison him, wherein we grant the defective the personal liberty to do as he pleases, until he pleases to descend to a plane of living below the animal level, and try to care for a few of his descendants who are so helpless that they can no longer exercise that personal liberty to do as they please,"—such a policy increases and multiplies the dangers of the over-fertile feeble-minded.[17]

The Mental Survey of the State of Oregon recently published by the United States Health Service, sets an excellent example and should be followed by every state in the Union and every civilized country as well. It is greatly to the credit of the Western State that it is one of the first officially to recognize the primary importance of this problem and to realize that facts, no matter how fatal to self-satisfaction, must be faced. This survey, authorized by the state legislature, and carried out by the University of Oregon, in collaboration with Dr. C. L. Carlisle of the Public Health service, aided by a large number of volunteers, shows that only a small percentage of mental defectives and morons are in the care of institutions. The rest are widely scattered and their condition unknown or neglected. They are docile and submissive, they do not attract attention to themselves as do the criminal delinquents and the insane. Nevertheless, it is estimated that they number no less than 75,000 men, women, and children, out of a total population of 783,000, or about ten per cent. Oregon, it is thought, is no exception to other states. Yet under our present conditions, these people are actually encouraged to increase and multiply and replenish the earth.

Concerning the importance of the Oregon survey, we may quote Surgeon General H. C. Cumming: "the prevention and correction of mental defectives is one of the great public health problems of to-day. It enters into many phases of our work and its influence continually crops up unexpectedly. For instance, work of the Public Health Service in connection with juvenile courts shows that a marked proportion of juvenile delinquency is traceable to some degree of mental deficiency in the offender. For years Public Health officials have concerned themselves only with the disorders of physical health; but now they are realizing the significance of mental health also. The work in Oregon constitutes the first state-wide survey which even begins to disclose the enormous drain on a state, caused by mental defects. One of the objects of the work was to obtain for the people of Oregon an idea of the problem that confronted them and the heavy annual loss, both economic and industrial, that it entailed. Another was to enable the legislators to devise a program that

---

[17] Dwellers in the Vale of Siddem: A True Story of the Social Aspect of Feeble-mindedness. By A. C. Rogers and Maud A. Merrill; Boston (1919).

would stop much of the loss, restore to health and bring to lives of industrial usefulness, many of those now down and out, and above all, to save hundreds of children from growing up to lives of misery."

It will be interesting to see how many of our State Legislatures have the intelligence and the courage to follow in the footsteps of Oregon in this respect. Nothing could more effectually stimulate discussion, and awaken intelligence as to the extravagance and cost to the community of our present codes of traditional morality. But we should make sure in all such surveys, that mental defect is not concealed even in such dignified bodies as state legislatures and among those leaders who are urging men and women to reckless and irresponsible procreation.

I have touched upon these various aspects of the complex problem of the feeble-minded, and the menace of the moron to human society, not merely for the purpose of reiterating that it is one of the greatest and most difficult social problems of modern times, demanding an immediate, stern and definite policy, but because it illustrates the actual harvest of reliance upon traditional morality, upon the biblical injunction to increase and multiply, a policy still taught by politician, priest and militarist. Motherhood has been held universally sacred; yet, as Bouchacourt pointed out, "to-day, the dregs of the human species, the blind, the deaf-mute, the degenerate, the nervous, the vicious, the idiotic, the imbecile, the cretins and the epileptics—are better protected than pregnant women." The syphilitic, the irresponsible, the feeble-minded are encouraged to breed unhindered, while all the powerful forces of tradition, of custom, or prejudice, have bolstered up the desperate effort to block the inevitable influence of true civilization in spreading the principles of independence, self-reliance, discrimination and foresight upon which the great practice of intelligent parenthood is based.

To-day we are confronted by the results of this official policy. There is no escaping it; there is no explaining it away. Surely it is an amazing and discouraging phenomenon that the very governments that have seen fit to interfere in practically every phase of the normal citizen's life, dare not attempt to restrain, either by force or persuasion, the moron and the imbecile from producing his large family of feeble-minded offspring.

In my own experience, I recall vividly the case of a feeble-minded girl who every year, for a long period, received the expert attention of a great specialist in one of the best-known maternity hospitals of New York City. The great obstetrician, for the benefit of interns and medical students, performed each year a Caesarian operation upon this unfortunate creature to bring into the world her defective, and, in one case at least, her syphilitic, infant. "Nelly" was then sent to a special room and placed under the care of a day nurse and a night nurse, with extra and special nourishment provided. Each year she returned to the hospital. Such cases are not exceptions; any experienced doctor or nurse can recount similar stories. In the interest of medical science this practice may be justified. I am not criticising it from that point of view. I realize as well as the most conservative moralist that humanity requires that healthy members of the race should make certain sacrifices to preserve from death those unfortunates who are born with hereditary taints. But there is a point at which philanthropy may become positively dysgenic, when charity is converted into injustice to the self-supporting citizen, into positive injury to the future of the race. Such a point, it seems obvious, is reached when the incurably defective are permitted to procreate and thus increase their numbers.

The problem of the dependent, delinquent and defective elements in modern society, we must repeat, cannot be minimized because of their alleged small numerical proportion to the rest of the population. The proportion seems small only because we accustom ourselves to the habit of looking upon feeble-mindedness as a separate and distinct calamity to the race, as a chance phenomenon unrelated to the sexual and biological customs not only condoned but even encouraged by our so-called civilization. The actual dangers can only be fully realized when we have acquired definite information concerning the financial and cultural cost of these classes to the community, when we become fully cognizant of the burden of the imbecile upon the whole human race; when we see the funds that should be available for human development, for scientific, artistic and philosophic research, being diverted annually, by hundreds of millions of dollars, to the care and segregation of men, women, and children who never should have been born. The advocate of Birth Control realizes as well as all intelligent thinkers the dangers of interfering with personal liberty. Our whole philosophy is, in fact, based upon the fundamental assumption that man is a self-conscious, self-governing creature, that he should not be treated as a domestic animal; that he must be left free, at least within certain wide limits, to follow his own wishes in the matter of mating and in the procreation of children. Nor do we believe that the community could or should send to the lethal chamber the defective progeny resulting from irresponsible and unintelligent breeding.

But modern society, which has respected the personal liberty of the individual only in regard to the unrestricted and irresponsible bringing into the world of filth and poverty an overcrowding procession of infants foredoomed to death or hereditable disease, is now confronted with the problem of protecting itself and its future generations against the inevitable consequences of this long-practised policy of *laisser-faire*.

The emergency problem of segregation and sterilization must be faced immediately. Every feeble-minded girl or woman of the hereditary type, especially of the moron class, should be segregated during the reproductive period. Otherwise, she is almost certain to bear imbecile children, who in turn are just as certain to breed other defectives. The male defectives are no less dangerous. Segregation carried out for one or two generations would give us only partial control of the problem. Moreover, when we realize that each feeble-minded person is a potential source of an endless progeny of defect, we prefer the policy of immediate sterilization, of making sure that parenthood is absolutely prohibited to the feeble-minded.

This, I say, is an emergency measure. But how are we to prevent the repetition in the future of a new harvest of imbecility, the recurrence of new generations of morons and defectives, as the logical and inevitable consequence of the universal application of the traditional and widely approved command to increase and multiply?

At the present moment, we are offered three distinct and more or less mutually exclusive policies by which civilization may hope to protect itself and the generations of the future from the allied dangers of imbecility, defect and delinquency. No one can understand the necessity for Birth Control education without a complete comprehension of the dangers, the inadequacies, or the limitations of the present attempts at control, or the proposed programs for social reconstruction and racial regeneration. It is, therefore, necessary to interpret and criticize the three programs offered to meet our emergency. These may be briefly summarized as follows:

(1) Philanthropy and Charity: This is the present and traditional method of meeting the problems of human defect and dependence, of poverty and delinquency. It is emotional, altruistic, at best ameliorative, aiming to meet the individual situation as it arises and presents itself. Its effect in practise is seldom, if ever, truly preventive. Concerned with symptoms, with the allaying of acute and catastrophic miseries, it cannot, if it would, strike at the radical causes of social misery. At its worst, it is sentimental and paternalistic.

(2) Marxian Socialism: This may be considered typical of many widely varying schemes of more or less revolutionary social reconstruction, emphasizing the primary importance of environment, education, equal opportunity, and health, in the elimination of the conditions (i. e. capitalistic control of industry) which have resulted in biological chaos and human waste. I shall attempt to show that the Marxian doctrine is both too limited, too superficial and too fragmentary in its basic analysis of human nature and in its program of revolutionary reconstruction.

(3) Eugenics: Eugenics seems to me to be valuable in its critical and diagnostic aspects, in emphasizing the danger of irresponsible and uncontrolled fertility of the "unfit" and the feeble-minded establishing a progressive unbalance in human society and lowering the birth-rate among the "fit." But in its so-called "constructive" aspect, in seeking to reestablish the dominance of healthy strain over the unhealthy, by urging an increased birth-rate among the fit, the Eugenists really offer nothing more farsighted than a "cradle competition" between the fit and the unfit. They suggest in very truth, that all intelligent and respectable parents should take as their example in this grave matter of child-bearing the most irresponsible elements in the community.

CHAPTER V: The Cruelty of Charity

"Fostering the good-for-nothing at the expense of the good is an extreme cruelty. It is a deliberate storing up of miseries for future generations. There is no greater curse to posterity than that of bequeathing them an increasing population of imbeciles."

Herbert Spencer

The last century has witnessed the rise and development of philanthropy and organized charity. Coincident with the all-conquering power of machinery and capitalistic control, with the unprecedented growth of great cities and industrial centers, and the creation of great proletarian populations, modern civilization has been confronted, to a degree hitherto unknown in human history, with the complex problem of sustaining human life in surroundings and under conditions flagrantly dysgenic.

The program, as I believe all competent authorities in contemporary philanthropy and organized charity would agree, has been altered in aim and purpose. It was first the outgrowth of humanitarian and altruistic idealism, perhaps not devoid of a strain of sentimentalism, of an idealism that was aroused by a desperate picture of human misery intensified by the industrial revolution. It has developed in later years into a program not so much aiming to succor the unfortunate victims of circumstances, as to effect what we may term social sanitation. Primarily, it is a program of self-protection. Contemporary philanthropy, I believe, recognizes that extreme poverty and overcrowded slums are veritable breeding-grounds of epidemics, disease, delinquency and dependency. Its aim, therefore, is to prevent the individual family from sinking to that abject condition in which it will become a much heavier burden upon society.

There is no need here to criticize the obvious limitations of organized charities in meeting the desperate problem of destitution. We are all familiar with these criticisms: the common indictment of "inefficiency" so often brought against public and privately endowed agencies. The charges include the high cost of administration; the pauperization of deserving poor, and the encouragement and fostering of the "undeserving"; the progressive destruction of self-respect and self-reliance by the paternalistic interference of social agencies; the impossibility of keeping pace with the ever-increasing multiplication of factors and influences responsible for the perpetuation of human misery; the misdirection and misappropriation of endowments; the absence of inter-organization and coordination of the various agencies of church, state, and privately endowed institutions; the "crimes of charity" that are occasionally exposed in newspaper scandals. These and similar strictures we may ignore as irrelevant to our present purpose, as inevitable but not

40

incurable faults that have been and are being eliminated in the slow but certain growth of a beneficent power in modern civilization. In reply to such criticisms, the protagonist of modern philanthropy might justly point to the honest and sincere workers and disinterested scientists it has mobilized, to the self-sacrificing and hard-working executives who have awakened public attention to the evils of poverty and the menace to the race engendered by misery and filth.

Even if we accept organized charity at its own valuation, and grant that it does the best it can, it is exposed to a more profound criticism. It reveals a fundamental and irremediable defect. Its very success, its very efficiency, its very necessity to the social order, are themselves the most unanswerable indictment. Organized charity itself is the symptom of a malignant social disease.

Those vast, complex, interrelated organizations aiming to control and to diminish the spread of misery and destitution and all the menacing evils that spring out of this sinisterly fertile soil, are the surest sign that our civilization has bred, is breeding and is perpetuating constantly increasing numbers of defectives, delinquents and dependents. My criticism, therefore, is not directed at the "failure" of philanthropy, but rather at its success.

These dangers inherent in the very idea of humanitarianism and altruism, dangers which have to-day produced their full harvest of human waste, of inequality and inefficiency, were fully recognized in the last century at the moment when such ideas were first put into practice. Readers of Huxley's attack on the Salvation Army will recall his penetrating and stimulating condemnation of the debauch of sentimentalism which expressed itself in so uncontrolled a fashion in the Victorian era. One of the most penetrating of American thinkers, Henry James, Sr., sixty or seventy years ago wrote: "I have been so long accustomed to see the most arrant deviltry transact itself in the name of benevolence, that the moment I hear a profession of good will from almost any quarter, I instinctively look around for a constable or place my hand within reach of a bell-rope. My ideal of human intercourse would be a state of things in which no man will ever stand in need of any other man's help, but will derive all his satisfaction from the great social tides which own no individual names. I am sure no man can be put in a position of dependence upon another, without the other's very soon becoming—if he accepts the duties of the relation—utterly degraded out of his just human proportions. No man can play the Deity to his fellow man with impunity—I mean, spiritual impunity, of course. For see: if I am at all satisfied with that relation, if it contents me to be in a position of generosity towards others, I must be remarkably indifferent at bottom to the gross social inequality which permits that position, and, instead of resenting the enforced humiliation of my fellow man to myself in the interests of humanity, I acquiesce in it for the sake of the profit it yields to my own self-complacency. I do hope the reign of benevolence is over; until that event occurs, I am sure the reign of God will be impossible."

To-day, we may measure the evil effects of "benevolence" of this type, not merely upon those who have indulged in it, but upon the community at large. These effects have been reduced to statistics and we cannot, if we would, escape their significance. Look, for instance (since they are close at hand, and fairly representative of conditions elsewhere) at the total annual expenditures of public and private "charities and corrections" for the State of New York. For the year ending June 30, 1919, the expenditures of public institutions and agencies amounted to $33, 936,205.88. The expenditures of privately supported and endowed institutions for the same year, amount to $58,100,530.98. This makes a total, for public and private charities and corrections of $92,036,736.86. A conservative estimate of the increase for the year (1920-1921) brings this figure approximately to one-hundred and twenty-five millions. These figures take on an eloquent significance if we compare them to the comparatively small amounts spent upon education, conservation of health and other constructive efforts. Thus, while the City of New York spent $7.35 per capita on public education in the year 1918, it spent on public charities no less than $2.66. Add to this last figure an even larger amount dispensed by private agencies, and we may derive some definite sense of the heavy burden of dependency, pauperism and delinquency upon the normal and healthy sections of the community.

Statistics now available also inform us that more than a million dollars are spent annually to support the public and private institutions in the state of New York for the segregation of the feeble-minded and the epileptic. A million and a half is spent for the up-keep of state prisons, those homes of the "defective delinquent." Insanity, which, we should remember, is to a great extent hereditary, annually drains from the state treasury no less than $11,985,695.55, and from private sources and endowments another twenty millions. When we learn further that the total number of inmates in public and private institutions in the State of New York—in alms-houses, reformatories, schools for the blind, deaf and mute, in insane asylums, in homes for the feeble-minded and epileptic—amounts practically to less than sixty-five thousand, an insignificant number compared to the total population, our eyes should be opened to the terrific cost to the community of this dead weight of human waste.

The United States Public Health Survey of the State of Oregon, recently published, shows that even a young community, rich in natural resources, and unusually progressive in legislative measures, is no less subject to this burden. Out of a total population of 783,000 it is estimated that more than 75,000 men, women and children are dependents, feeble-minded, or delinquents. Thus about 10 per cent. of the population is a constant drain on the finances, health, and future of that community. These figures represent a more definite and precise survey than the rough one indicated by the statistics of charities and correction for the State of New York. The figures yielded by this Oregon survey are also considerably lower than the average shown by the draft examination, a fact which indicates that they are not higher than might be obtained from other States.

Organized charity is thus confronted with the problem of feeble-mindedness and mental defect. But just as the State has so far neglected the problem of mental defect until this takes the form of criminal delinquency, so the tendency of our philanthropic and charitable agencies has been to pay no attention to the problem until it has expressed itself in terms of pauperism and delinquency. Such "benevolence" is not merely ineffectual; it is positively injurious to the community and the future of the race.

But there is a special type of philanthropy or benevolence, now widely advertised and advocated, both as a federal program and as worthy of private endowment, which strikes me as being more insidiously injurious than any other. This concerns itself directly with the function of maternity, and aims to supply *gratis* medical and nursing facilities to slum mothers. Such women are to be visited by nurses and to receive instruction in the "hygiene of pregnancy"; to be guided in making arrangements for confinements; to be invited to come to the doctor's clinics for examination and supervision. They are, we are informed, to "receive adequate care during pregnancy, at confinement, and for one month afterward." Thus are mothers and babies to be saved. "Childbearing is to be made safe." The work of the maternity centers in the various American cities in which they have already been established and in which they are supported by private contributions and endowment, it is hardly necessary to point out, is carried on among the poor and more docile sections of the city, among mothers least able, through poverty and ignorance, to afford the care and attention necessary for successful maternity. Now, as the findings of Tredgold and Karl Pearson and the British Eugenists so conclusively show, and as the infant mortality reports so thoroughly substantiate, a high rate of fecundity is always associated with the direst poverty, irresponsibility, mental defect, feeble-mindedness, and other transmissible taints. The effect of maternity endowments and maternity centers supported by private philanthropy would have, perhaps already have had, exactly the most dysgenic tendency. The new government program would facilitate the function of maternity among the very classes in which the absolute necessity is to discourage it.

Such "benevolence" is not merely superficial and near-sighted. It conceals a stupid cruelty, because it is not courageous enough to face unpleasant facts. Aside from the question of the unfitness of many women to become mothers, aside from the very definite deterioration in the human stock that such programs would inevitably hasten, we may question its value even to the normal though unfortunate mother. For it is never the intention of such philanthropy to give the poor over-burdened and often undernourished mother of the slum the opportunity to make the choice herself, to decide whether she wishes time after to time to bring children into the world. It merely says "Increase and multiply: We are prepared to help you do this." Whereas the great majority of mothers realize the grave responsibility they face in keeping alive and rearing the children they have already brought into the world, the maternity center would teach them how to have more. The poor woman is taught how to have her seventh child, when what she wants to know is how to avoid bringing into the world her eighth.

Such philanthropy, as Dean Inge has so unanswerably pointed out, is kind only to be cruel, and unwittingly promotes precisely the results most deprecated. It encourages the healthier and more normal sections of the world to shoulder the burden of unthinking and indiscriminate fecundity of others; which brings with it, as I think the reader must agree, a dead weight of human waste. Instead of decreasing and aiming to eliminate the stocks that are most detrimental to the future of the race and the world, it tends to render them to a menacing degree dominant.

On the other hand, the program is an indication of a suddenly awakened public recognition of the shocking conditions surrounding pregnancy, maternity, and infant welfare prevailing at the very heart of our boasted civilization. So terrible, so unbelievable, are these conditions of child-bearing, degraded far below the level of primitive and barbarian tribes, nay, even below the plane of brutes, that many high-minded people, confronted with such revolting and disgraceful facts, lost that calmness of vision and impartiality of judgment so necessary in any serious consideration of this vital problem. Their "hearts" are touched; they become hysterical; they demand immediate action; and enthusiastically and generously they support the first superficial program that is advanced. Immediate action may sometimes be worse than no action at all. The "warm heart" needs the balance of the cool head. Much harm has been done in the world by those too-good-hearted folk who have always demanded that "something be done at once."

They do not stop to consider that the very first thing to be done is to subject the whole situation to the deepest and most rigorous thinking. As the late Walter Bagehot wrote in a significant but too often forgotten passage:

"The most melancholy of human reflections, perhaps, is that on the whole it is a question whether the benevolence of mankind does more good or harm. Great good, no doubt, philanthropy does, but then it also does great evil. It augments so much vice, it multiplies so much suffering, it brings to life such great populations to suffer and to be vicious, that it is open to argument whether it be or be not an evil to the world, and this is entirely because excellent people fancy they can do much by rapid action, and that they will most benefit the world when they most relieve their own feelings; that as soon as an evil is seen, 'something' ought to be done to stay and prevent it. One may incline to hope that the balance of good over evil is in favor of benevolence; one can hardly bear to think that it is not so; but anyhow it is certain that there is a most heavy debt of evil, and that this burden might almost all have been spared us if philanthropists as well as others had not inherited from their barbarous forefathers a wild passion for instant action."

It is customary, I believe, to defend philanthropy and charity upon the basis of the sanctity of human life. Yet recent events in the world reveal a curious contradiction in this respect. Human life is held sacred, as a general Christian principle, until war is declared, when humanity indulges in a universal debauch of bloodshed and barbarism, inventing poison gases and every type of diabolic suggestion to facilitate killing and starvation. Blockades are enforced to weaken and starve civilian populations—women and children. This accomplished, the pendulum of mob passion swings back to the opposite extreme, and the compensatory emotions express themselves in hysterical fashion. Philanthropy and charity are then unleashed. We begin to hold human life sacred again. We try to save the lives of the people we formerly sought to weaken by devastation, disease and starvation. We indulge in "drives," in campaigns of relief, in a general orgy of international charity.

We are thus witnessing to-day the inauguration of a vast system of international charity. As in our more limited communities and cities, where self-sustaining and self-reliant sections of the population are forced to shoulder the burden of the reckless and irresponsible, so in the great world community the more prosperous and incidentally less populous nations are asked to relieve and succor those countries which are either the victims of the wide-spread havoc of war, of militaristic statesmanship, or of the age-long tradition of reckless propagation and its consequent over-population.

The people of the United States have recently been called upon to exercise their traditional generosity not merely to aid the European Relief Council in its efforts to keep alive three million, five hundred thousand starving children in Central Europe, but in addition to contribute to that enormous fund to save the thirty million Chinese who find themselves at the verge of starvation, owing to one of those recurrent famines which strike often at that densely populated and inert country, where procreative recklessness is encouraged as a matter of duty. The results of this international charity have not justified the effort nor repaid the generosity to which it appealed. In the first place, no effort was made to prevent the recurrence of the disaster; in the second place, philanthropy of this type attempts to sweep back the tide of miseries created by unrestricted propagation, with the feeble broom of sentiment. As one of the most observant and impartial of authorities on the Far East, J. O. P. Bland, has pointed out: "So long as China maintains a birth-rate that is estimated at fifty-five per thousand or more, the only possible alternative to these visitations would be emigration and this would have to be on such a scale as would speedily overrun and overfill the habitable globe. Neither humanitarian schemes, international charities nor philanthropies can prevent widespread disaster to a people which habitually breeds up to and beyond the maximum limits of its food supply." Upon this point, it is interesting to add, Mr. Frank

A. Vanderlip has likewise pointed out the inefficacy and misdirection of this type of international charity.[18]

Mr. Bland further points out: "The problem presented is one with which neither humanitarian nor religious zeal can ever cope, so long as we fail to recognize and attack the fundamental cause of these calamities. As a matter of sober fact, the benevolent activities of our missionary societies to reduce the deathrate by the prevention of infanticide and the checking of disease, actually serve in the end to aggravate the pressure of population upon its food-supply and to increase the severity of the inevitably resultant catastrophe. What is needed for the prevention, or, at least, the mitigation of these scourges, is an organized educational propaganda, directed first against polygamy and the marriage of minors and the unfit, and, next, toward such a limitation of the birth-rate as shall approximate the standard of civilized countries. But so long as Bishops and well meaning philanthropists in England and America continue to praise and encourage `the glorious fertility of the East' there can be but little hope of minimizing the penalties of the ruthless struggle for existence in China, and Nature's law will therefore continue to work out its own pitiless solution, weeding out every year millions of predestined weaklings."

This rapid survey is enough, I hope, to indicate the manifold inadequacies inherent in present policies of philanthropy and charity. The most serious charge that can be brought against modern "benevolence" is that it encourages the perpetuation of defectives, delinquents and dependents. These are the most dangerous elements in the world community, the most devastating curse on human progress and expression. Philanthropy is a gesture characteristic of modern business lavishing upon the unfit the profits extorted from the community at large. Looked at impartially, this compensatory generosity is in its final effect probably more dangerous, more dysgenic, more blighting than the initial practice of profiteering and the social injustice which makes some too rich and others too poor.

---

[18] Birth Control Review. Vol. V. No. 4. p. 7.

CHAPTER VI: Neglected Factors of the World Problem

War has thrust upon us a new internationalism. To-day the world is united by starvation, disease and misery. We are enjoying the ironic internationalism of hatred. The victors are forced to shoulder the burden of the vanquished. International philanthropies and charities are organized. The great flux of immigration and emigration has recommenced. Prosperity is a myth; and the rich are called upon to support huge philanthropies, in the futile attempt to sweep back the tide of famine and misery. In the face of this new internationalism, this tangled unity of the world, all proposed political and economic programs reveal a woeful common bankruptcy. They are fragmentary and superficial. None of them go to the root of this unprecedented world problem. Politicians offer political solutions,—like the League of Nations or the limitation of navies. Militarists offer new schemes of competitive armament. Marxians offer the Third Internationale and industrial revolution. Sentimentalists offer charity and philanthropy. Coordination or correlation is lacking. And matters go steadily from bad to worse.

The first essential in the solution of any problem is the recognition and statement of the factors involved. Now in this complex problem which to-day confronts us, no attempt has been made to state the primary facts. The statesman believes they are all political. Militarists believe they are all military and naval. Economists, including under the term the various schools for Socialists, believe they are industrial and financial. Churchmen look upon them as religious and ethical. What is lacking is the recognition of that fundamental factor which reflects and coordinates these essential but incomplete phases of the problem,—the factor of reproduction. For in all problems affecting the welfare of a biological species, and particularly in all problems of human welfare, two fundamental forces work against each other. There is hunger as the driving force of all our economic, industrial and commercial organizations; and there is the reproductive impulse in continual conflict with our economic, political settlements, race adjustments and the like. Official moralists, statesmen, politicians, philanthropists and economists display an astounding disregard of this second disorganizing factor. They treat the world of men as if it were purely a hunger world instead of a hunger-sex world. Yet there is no phase of human society, no question of politics, economics, or industry that is not tied up in almost equal measure with the expression of both of these primordial impulses. You cannot sweep back overpowering dynamic instincts by catchwords. You can neglect and thwart sex only at your peril. You cannot solve the problem of hunger and ignore the problem of sex. They are bound up together.

While the gravest attention is paid to the problem of hunger and food, that of sex is neglected. Politicians and scientists are ready and willing to speak of such things as a "high birth rate," infant mortality, the dangers of immigration or over-population. But with few exceptions they cannot bring themselves to speak of Birth Control. Until they shall have broken through the traditional inhibitions concerning the discussion of sexual matters, until they recognize the force of the sexual instinct, and until they recognize Birth Control as the *pivotal factor* in the problem confronting the world to-day, our statesmen must continue to work in the dark. Political palliatives will be mocked by actuality. Economic nostrums are blown willy-nilly in the unending battle of human instincts.

A brief survey of the past three or four centuries of Western civilization suggests the urgent need of a new science to help humanity in the struggle with the vast problem of to-day's disorder and danger. That problem, as we envisage it, is fundamentally a sexual problem. Ethical, political, and economic avenues of approach are insufficient. We must create a new instrument, a new technique to make any adequate solution possible.

The history of the industrial revolution and the dominance of all-conquering machinery in Western civilization show the inadequacy of political and economic measures to meet the terrific rise in population. The advent of the factory system, due especially to the development of machinery at the beginning of the nineteenth century, upset all the grandiloquent theories of the previous era. To meet the new situation created by the industrial revolution arose the new science of "political economy," or economics. Old political methods proved inadequate to keep pace with the problem presented by the rapid rise of the new machine and industrial power. The machine era very shortly and decisively exploded the simple belief that "all men are born free and equal." Political power was superseded by economic and industrial power. To sustain their supremacy in the political field, governments and politicians allied themselves to the new industrial oligarchy. Old political theories and practices were totally inadequate to control the new situation or to meet the complex problems that grew out of it.

Just as the eighteenth century saw the rise and proliferation of political theories, the nineteenth witnessed the creation and development of the science of economics, which aimed to perfect an instrument for the study and analysis of an industrial society, and to offer a technique for the solution of the multifold problems it presented. But at the present moment, as the outcome of the machine era and competitive populations, the world has been thrown into a new situation, the solution of which is impossible solely by political or economic weapons.

The industrial revolution and the development of machinery in Europe and America called into being a new type of working-class. Machines were at first termed "labor-saving devices." In reality, as we now know, mechanical inventions and discoveries created unprecedented and increasingly enormous demand for "labor." The omnipresent and still existing scandal of child labor is ample evidence of this. Machine production in its opening phases, demanded large, concentrated and exploitable populations. Large production and the huge development of international trade through improved methods of transport, made possible the maintenance upon a low level of existence of these rapidly increasing proletarian populations. With the rise and spread throughout Europe and America of machine production, it is now possible to correlate the expansion of the "proletariat." The working-classes bred almost automatically to meet the demand for machine-serving "hands."

The rise in population, the multiplication of proletarian populations as a first result of mechanical industry, the appearance of great centers of population, the so-called urban drift, and the evils of overcrowding still remain insufficiently studied and stated. It is a significant though neglected fact that when, after long agitation in Great Britain, child labor was finally forbidden by law, the supply of children dropped appreciably. No longer of economic value in the factory, children were evidently a drug in the "home." Yet it is doubly significant that from this moment British labor began the long unending task of self-organization.[19]

Nineteenth century economics had no method of studying the interrelation of the biological factors with the industrial. Overcrowding, overwork, the progressive destruction of responsibility by the machine discipline, as is now perfectly obvious, had the most disastrous consequences upon human character and human habits.[20] Paternalistic philanthropies and sentimental charities, which sprang up like mushrooms, only tended to increase the evils of indiscriminate breeding. From the physiological and psychological point of view, the factory system has been nothing less than catastrophic.

Dr. Austin Freeman has recently pointed out[21] some of the physiological, psychological, and racial effects of machinery upon the proletariat, the breeders of the world. Speaking for Great Britain, Dr. Freeman suggests that the omnipresence of machinery tends toward the production of large but inferior populations. Evidences of biological and racial degeneracy are apparent to this observer. "Compared with the African negro," he writes, "the British sub-man is in several respects markedly inferior. He tends to be dull; he is usually quite helpless and unhandy; he has, as a rule, no skill or knowledge of handicraft, or indeed knowledge of any kind.... Over-population is a phenomenon connected with the survival of the unfit, and it is mechanism which has created conditions favorable to the survival of the unfit and the elimination of the fit." The whole indictment against machinery is summarized by Dr. Freeman: "Mechanism by its reactions on man and his

---

[19] It may be well to note, in this connection, that the decline in the birth rate among the more intelligent classes of British labor followed upon the famous Bradlaugh-Besant trial of 1878, the outcome of the attempt of these two courageous Birth Control pioneers to circulate among the workers the work of an American physician, Dr. Knowlton's "The Fruits of Philosophy," advocating Birth Control, and the widespread publicity resulting from his trial.

[20] Cf. The Creative Impulse in Industry, by Helen Marot. The Instinct of Workmanship, by Thorstein Veblen.

[21] Social Decay and Regeneration. By R. Austin Freeman. London 1921.

environment is antagonistic to human welfare. It has destroyed industry and replaced it by mere labor; it has degraded and vulgarized the works of man; it has destroyed social unity and replaced it by social disintegration and class antagonism to an extent which directly threatens civilization; it has injuriously affected the structural type of society by developing its organization at the expense of the individual; it has endowed the inferior man with political power which he employs to the common disadvantage by creating political institutions of a socially destructive type; and finally by its reactions on the activities of war it constitutes an agent for the wholesale physical destruction of man and his works and the extinction of human culture."

It is not necessary to be in absolute agreement with this diagnostician to realize the menace of machinery, which tends to emphasize quantity and mere number at the expense of quality and individuality. One thing is certain. If machinery is detrimental to biological fitness, the machine must be destroyed, as it was in Samuel Butler's "Erewhon." But perhaps there is another way of mastering this problem.

Altruism, humanitarianism and philanthropy have aided and abetted machinery in the destruction of responsibility and self-reliance among the least desirable elements of the proletariat. In contrast with the previous epoch of discovery of the New World, of exploration and colonization, when a centrifugal influence was at work upon the populations of Europe, the advent of machinery has brought with it a counteracting centripetal effect. The result has been the accumulation of large urban populations, the increase of irresponsibility, and ever-widening margin of biological waste.

Just as eighteenth century politics and political theories were unable to keep pace with the economic and capitalistic aggressions of the nineteenth century, so also we find, if we look closely enough, that nineteenth century economics is inadequate to lead the world out of the catastrophic situation into which it has been thrown by the debacle of the World War. Economists are coming to recognize that the purely economic interpretation of contemporary events is insufficient. Too long, as one of them has stated, orthodox economists have overlooked the important fact that "human life is dynamic, that change, movement, evolution, are its basic characteristics; that self-expression, and therefore freedom of choice and movement, are prerequisites to a satisfying human state".[22]

Economists themselves are breaking with the old "dismal science" of the Manchester school, with its sterile study of "supply and demand," of prices and exchange, of wealth and labor. Like the Chicago Vice Commission, nineteenth-century economists (many of whom still survive into our own day) considered sex merely as something to be legislated out of existence. They had the right idea that wealth consisted solely of material things used to promote the welfare of certain human beings. Their idea of capital was

---

[22] Carlton H. Parker: The Casual Laborer and other essays: p. 30.

somewhat confused. They apparently decided that capital was merely that part of capital used to produce profit. Prices, exchanges, commercial statistics, and financial operations comprised the subject matter of these older economists. It would have been considered "unscientific" to take into account the human factors involved. They might study the wear-and-tear and depreciation of machinery: but the depreciation or destruction of the human race did not concern them. Under "wealth" they never included the vast, wasted treasury of human life and human expression.

Economists to-day are awake to the imperative duty of dealing with the whole of human nature, with the relation of men, women, and children to their environment—physical and psychic as well as social; of dealing with all those factors which contribute to human sustenance, happiness and welfare. The economist, at length, investigates human motives. Economics outgrows the outworn metaphysical preconceptions of nineteenth century theory. To-day we witness the creation of a new "welfare" or social economics, based on a fuller and more complete knowledge of the human race, upon a recognition of sex as well as of hunger; in brief, of physiological instincts and psychological demands. The newer economists are beginning to recognize that their science heretofore failed to take into account the most vital factors in modern industry—it failed to foresee the inevitable consequences of compulsory motherhood; the catastrophic effects of child labor upon racial health; the overwhelming importance of national vitality and well-being; the international ramifications of the population problem; the relation of indiscriminate breeding to feeble-mindedness, and industrial inefficiency. It speculated too little or not at all on human motives. Human nature riots through the traditional economic structure, as Carlton Parker pointed out, with ridicule and destruction; the old-fashioned economist looked on helpless and aghast.

Inevitably we are driven to the conclusion that the exhaustively economic interpretation of contemporary history is inadequate to meet the present situation. In his suggestive book, "The Acquisitive Society," R. H. Tawney, arrives at the conclusion that "obsession by economic issues is as local and transitory as it is repulsive and disturbing. To future generations it will appear as pitiable as the obsession of the seventeenth century by religious quarrels appears to-day; indeed, it is less rational, since the object with which it is concerned is less important. And it is a poison which inflames every wound and turns each trivial scratch into a malignant ulcer. Society will not solve the particular problems of industry until that poison is expelled, and it has learned to see industry in its proper perspective. *If it is to do that it must rearrange the scale of values.* It must regard economic interests as one element in life, not as the whole of life...."[23]

---

[23] R. H. Tawney. The Acquisitive Society, p. 184.

In neglecting or minimizing the great factor of sex in human society, the Marxian doctrine reveals itself as no stronger than orthodox economics in guiding our way to a sound civilization. It works within the same intellectual limitations. Much as we are indebted to the Marxians for pointing out the injustice of modern industrialism, we should never close our eyes to the obvious limitations of their own "economic interpretation of history." While we must recognize the great historical value of Marx, it is now evident that his vision of the "class struggle," of the bitter irreconcilable warfare between the capitalist and working classes was based not upon historical analysis, but upon on unconscious dramatization of a superficial aspect of capitalistic regime.

In emphasizing the conflict between the classes, Marx failed to recognize the deeper unity of the proletariat and the capitalist. Nineteenth century capitalism had in reality engendered and cultivated the very type of working class best suited to its own purpose—an inert, docile, irresponsible and submissive class, progressively incapable of effective and aggressive organization. Like the economists of the Manchester school, Marx failed to recognize the interplay of human instincts in the world of industry. All the virtues were embodied in the beloved proletariat; all the villainies in the capitalists. The greatest asset of the capitalism of that age was, as a matter of fact, the uncontrolled breeding among the laboring classes. The intelligent and self-conscious section of the workers was forced to bear the burden of the unemployed and the poverty-stricken.

Marx was fully aware of the consequences of this condition of things, but shut his eyes tightly to the cause. He pointed out that capitalistic power was dependent upon "the reserve army of labor," surplus labor, and a wide margin of unemployment. He practically admitted that over-population was the inevitable soil of predatory capitalism. But he disregarded the most obvious consequence of that admission. It was all very dramatic and grandiloquent to tell the workingmen of the world to unite, that they had "nothing but their chains to lose and the world to gain." Cohesion of any sort, united and voluntary organization, as events have proved, is impossible in populations bereft of intelligence, self-discipline and even the material necessities of life, and cheated by their desires and ignorance into unrestrained and uncontrolled fertility.

In pointing out the limitations and fallacies of the orthodox Marxian opinion, my purpose is not to depreciate the efforts of the Socialists aiming to create a new society, but rather to emphasize what seems to me the greatest and most neglected truth of our day:—Unless sexual science is incorporated as an integral part of world-statesmanship and the pivotal importance of Birth Control is recognized in any program of reconstruction, all efforts to create a new world and a new civilization are foredoomed to failure.

We can hope for no advance until we attain a new conception of sex, not as a merely propagative act, not merely as a biological necessity for the perpetuation of the race, but as a psychic and spiritual avenue of expression. It is the limited, inhibited conception of sex that vitiates so much of the thought and ideation of the Eugenists.

Like most of our social idealists, statesmen, politicians and economists, some of the Eugenists suffer intellectually from a restricted and inhibited understanding of the function of sex. This limited understanding, this narrowness of vision, which gives rise to most of the misconceptions and condemnations of the doctrine of Birth Control, is responsible or the failure of politicians and legislators to enact practical statutes or to remove traditional obscenities from the law books. The most encouraging sign at present is the recognition by modern psychology of the central importance of the sexual instinct in human society, and the rapid spread of this new concept among the more enlightened sections of the civilized communities. The new conception of sex has been well stated by one to whom the debt of contemporary civilization is well-nigh immeasurable. "Sexual activity," Havelock Ellis has written, "is not merely a baldly propagative act, nor, when propagation is put aside, is it merely the relief of distended vessels. It is something more even than the foundation of great social institutions. It is the function by which all the finer activities of the organism, physical and psychic, may be developed and satisfied."[24]

No less than seventy years ago, a profound but neglected thinker, George Drysdale, emphasized the necessity of a thorough understanding of man's sexual nature in approaching economic, political and social problems. "Before we can undertake the calm and impartial investigation of any social problem, we must first of all free ourselves from all those sexual prejudices which are so vehement and violent and which so completely distort our vision of the external world. Society as a whole has yet to fight its way through an almost impenetrable forest of sexual taboos." Drysdale's words have lost none of their truth even to-day: "There are few things from which humanity has suffered more than the degraded and irreverent feelings of mystery and shame that have been attached to the genital and excretory organs. The former have been regarded, like their corresponding mental passions, as something of a lower and baser nature, tending to degrade and carnalize man by their physical appetites. But we cannot take a debasing view of any part of our humanity without becoming degraded in our whole being."[25]

Drysdale moreover clearly recognized the social crime of entrusting to sexual barbarians the duty of legislating and enforcing laws detrimental to the welfare of all future generations. "They trust blindly to authority for the rules they blindly lay down," he wrote, "perfectly unaware of the awful and complicated nature of the subject they are dealing with so confidently and of the horrible evils their unconsidered statements are attended with. They

---

[24] Medical Review of Reviews: Vol. XXVI, p. 116.
[25] The Elements of Social Science: London, 1854.

themselves break through the most fundamentally important laws daily in utter unconsciousness of the misery they are causing to their fellows...."

Psychologists to-day courageously emphasize the integral relationship of the expression of the sexual instinct with every phase of human activity. Until we recognize this central fact, we cannot understand the implications and the sinister significance of superficial attempts to apply rosewater remedies to social evils,—by the enactment of restrictive and superficial legislation, by wholesale philanthropies and charities, by publicly burying our heads in the sands of sentimentality. Self-appointed censors, grossly immoral "moralists," makeshift legislators, all face a heavy responsibility for the miseries, diseases, and social evils they perpetuate or intensify by enforcing the primitive taboos of aboriginal customs, traditions, and outworn laws, which at every step hinder the education of the people in the scientific knowledge of their sexual nature. Puritanic and academic taboo of sex in education and religion is as disastrous to human welfare as prostitution or the venereal scourges. "We are compelled squarely to face the distorting influences of biologically aborted reformers as well as the wastefulness of seducers," Dr. Edward A. Kempf recently declared. "Man arose from the ape and inherited his passions, which he can only refine but dare not attempt to castrate unless he would destroy the fountains of energy that maintain civilization and make life worth living and the world worth beautifying.... We do not have a problem that is to be solved by making repressive laws and executing them. Nothing will be more disastrous. Society must make life worth the living and the refining for the individual by conditioning him to love and to seek the love-object in a manner that reflects a constructive effect upon his fellow-men and by giving him suitable opportunities. The virility of the automatic apparatus is destroyed by excessive gormandizing or hunger, by excessive wealth or poverty, by excessive work or idleness, by sexual abuse or intolerant prudishness. The noblest and most difficult art of all is the raising of human thoroughbreds."[26]

[26] Proceedings of the International Conference of Women Physicians. Vol. IV, pp. 66-67. New York, 1920.

CHAPTER VII: Is Revolution the Remedy?

Marxian Socialism, which seeks to solve the complex problem of human misery by economic and proletarian revolution, has manifested a new vitality. Every shade of Socialistic thought and philosophy acknowledges its indebtedness to the vision of Karl Marx and his conception of the class struggle. Yet the relation of Marxian Socialism to the philosophy of Birth Control, especially in the minds of most Socialists, remains hazy and confused. No thorough understanding of Birth Control, its aims and purposes, is possible until this confusion has been cleared away, and we come to a realization that Birth Control is not merely independent of, but even antagonistic to the Marxian dogma. In recent years many Socialists have embraced the doctrine of Birth Control, and have generously promised us that "under Socialism" voluntary motherhood will be adopted and popularized as part of a general educational system. We might more logically reply that no Socialism will ever be possible until the problem of responsible parenthood has been solved.

Many Socialists to-day remain ignorant of the inherent conflict between the idea of Birth Control and the philosophy of Marx. The earlier Marxians, including Karl Marx himself, expressed the bitterest antagonism to Malthusian and neo-Malthusian theories. A remarkable feature of early Marxian propaganda has been the almost complete unanimity with which the implications of the Malthusian doctrine have been derided, denounced and repudiated. Any defense of the so-called "law of population" was enough to stamp one, in the eyes of the orthodox Marxians, as a "tool of the capitalistic class," seeking to dampen the ardor of those who expressed the belief that men might create a better world for themselves. Malthus, they claimed, was actuated by selfish class motives. He was not merely a hidebound aristocrat, but a pessimist who was trying to kill all hope of human progress. By Marx, Engels, Bebel, Karl Kautsky, and all the celebrated leaders and interpreters of Marx's great "Bible of the working class," down to the martyred Rosa Luxemburg and Karl Liebknecht, Birth Control has been looked upon as a subtle, Machiavellian sophistry created for the purpose of placing the blame for human misery elsewhere than at the door of the capitalist class. Upon this point the orthodox Marxian mind has been universally and sternly uncompromising.

Marxian vituperation of Malthus and his followers is illuminating. It reveals not the weakness of the thinker attacked, but of the aggressor. This is nowhere more evident than in Marx's "Capital" itself. In that monumental effort, it is impossible to discover any adequate refutation or even calm discussion of the dangers of irresponsible parenthood and reckless breeding, any suspicion that this recklessness and irresponsibility is even remotely related to the miseries of the proletariat. Poor Malthus is there relegated to the humble level of a footnote. "If the reader reminds me of Malthus, whose essay on Population appeared in 1798," Marx remarks somewhat tartly, "I remind him that this work in its first form is nothing more than a schoolboyish, superficial plagiary of De Foe, Sir James Steuart, Townsend, Franklin, Wallace, etc., and does not contain a single sentence thought out by himself. The great sensation this pamphlet caused was due solely to party interest. The French Revolution had passionate defenders in the United Kingdom.... 'The Principles of Population' was quoted with jubilance by the English oligarchy as the great destroyer of all hankerings after human development."[27]

The only attempt that Marx makes here toward answering the theory of Malthus is to declare that most of the population theory teachers were merely Protestant parsons.—"Parson Wallace, Parson Townsend, Parson Malthus and his pupil the Arch-Parson Thomas Chalmers, to say nothing of the lesser reverend scribblers in this line." The great pioneer of "scientific" Socialism then proceeds to berate parsons as philosophers and economists, using this method of escape from the very pertinent question of surplus population and surplus proletariat in its relation to labor organization and unemployment. It is true that elsewhere[28] he goes so far as to admit that "even Malthus recognized over-population as a necessity of modern industry, though, after his narrow fashion, he explains it by the absolute over-growth of the laboring population, not by their becoming relatively supernumerary." A few pages later, however, Marx comes back again to the question of over-population, failing to realize that it is to the capitalists' advantage that the working classes are unceasingly prolific. "The folly is now patent," writes the unsuspecting Marx, "of the economic wisdom that preaches to the laborers the accommodation of their numbers to the requirements of capital. The mechanism of capitalist production and accumulation constantly affects this adjustment. The first work of this adaptation is the creation of a relatively surplus population or industrial reserve army. Its last work is the misery of constantly extending strata of the army of labor, and the dead weight of pauperism." A little later he ventures again in the direction of Malthusianism so far as to admit that "the accumulation of wealth at one pole is... at the same time the accumulation of misery, agony of toil, slavery, ignorance, brutality and mental degradation at the opposite pole." Nevertheless, there is no indication that Marx permitted himself to see that the proletariat accommodates its numbers to the "requirements of capital" precisely by breeding a large, docile, submissive and easily exploitable population.

Had the purpose of Marx been impartial and scientific, this trifling difference might easily have been overcome and the dangers of reckless breeding insisted upon. But beneath all this wordy pretension and economic jargon, we detect another aim. That is the unconscious dramatization of

---

[27] Marx: "Capital." Vol. I, p. 675.
[28] Op. cit. pp, 695, 707, 709.

human society into the "class conflict." Nothing was overlooked that might sharpen and accentuate this "conflict." Marx depicted a great melodramatic conflict, in which all the virtues were embodied in the proletariat and all the villainies in the capitalist. In the end, as always in such dramas, virtue was to be rewarded and villainy punished. The working class was the temporary victim of a subtle but thorough conspiracy of tyranny and repression. Capitalists, intellectuals and the *bourgeoisie* were all "in on" this diabolic conspiracy, all thoroughly familiar with the plot, which Marx was so sure he had uncovered. In the last act was to occur that catastrophic revolution, with the final transformation scene of the Socialist millennium. Presented in "scientific" phraseology, with all the authority of economic terms, "Capital" appeared at the psychological moment. The heaven of the traditional theology had been shattered by Darwinian science, and here, dressed up in all the authority of the new science, appeared a new theology, the promise of a new heaven, an earthly paradise, with an impressive scale of rewards for the faithful and ignominious punishments for the capitalists.

Critics have often been puzzled by the tremendous vitality of this work. Its predictions have never, despite the claims of the faithful, been fulfilled. Instead of diminishing, the spirit of nationalism has been intensified tenfold. In nearly every respect Marx's predictions concerning the evolution of historical and economic forces have been contradicted by events, culminating in the great war. Most of his followers, the "revolutionary" Socialists, were swept into the whirlpool of nationalistic militarism. Nevertheless, this "Bible of the working classes" still enjoys a tremendous authority as a scientific work. By some it is regarded as an economic treatise; by others as a philosophy of history; by others as a collection of sociological laws; and finally by others as a moral and political book of reference. Criticized, refuted, repudiated and demolished by specialists, it nevertheless exerts its influences and retains its mysterious vitality.

We must seek the explanation of this secret elsewhere. Modern psychology has taught us that human nature has a tendency to place the cause of its own deficiencies and weaknesses outside of itself, to attribute to some external agency, to some enemy or group of enemies, the blame for its own misery. In his great work Marx unconsciously strengthens and encourages this tendency. The immediate effect of his teaching, vulgarized and popularized in a hundred different forms, is to relieve the proletariat of all responsibility for the effects of its reckless breeding, and even to encourage it in the perpetuation of misery.

The inherent truth in the Marxian teachings was, moreover, immediately subordinated to their emotional and religious appeal. A book that could so influence European thought could not be without merit. But in the process of becoming the "Bible of the working classes," "Capital" suffered the fate of all such "Bibles." The spirit of ecclesiastical dogmatism was transfused into the religion of revolutionary Socialism. This dogmatic religious quality has been noted by many of the most observant critics of Socialism. Marx was too readily accepted as the father of the church, and "Capital" as the sacred gospel of the social revolution. All questions of tactics, of propaganda, of class warfare, of political policy, were to be solved by apt quotations from the "good book." New thoughts, new schemes, new programs, based upon tested fact and experience, the outgrowth of newer discoveries concerning the nature of men, upon the recognition of the mistakes of the master, could only be approved or admitted according as they could or could not be tested by some bit of text quoted from Marx. His followers assumed that Karl Marx had completed the philosophy of Socialism, and that the duty of the proletariat thenceforth was not to think for itself, but merely to mobilize itself under competent Marxian leaders for the realization of his ideas.

From the day of this apotheosis of Marx until our own, the "orthodox" Socialist of any shade is of the belief that the first essential for social salvation lies in unquestioning belief in the dogmas of Marx.

The curious and persistent antagonism to Birth Control that began with Marx and continues to our own day can be explained only as the utter refusal or inability to consider humanity in its physiological and psychological aspects—these aspects, apparently, having no place in the "economic interpretation of history." It has remained for George Bernard Shaw, a Socialist with a keener spiritual insight than the ordinary Marxist, to point out the disastrous consequences of rapid multiplication which are obvious to the small cultivator, the peasant proprietor, the lowest farmhand himself, but which seem to arouse the orthodox, intellectual Marxian to inordinate fury. "But indeed the more you degrade the workers," Shaw once wrote,[29] "robbing them of all artistic enjoyment, and all chance of respect and admiration from their fellows, the more you throw them back, reckless, upon the one pleasure and the one human tie left to them—the gratification of their instinct for producing fresh supplies of men. You will applaud this instinct as divine until at last the excessive supply becomes a nuisance: there comes a plague of men; and you suddenly discover that the instinct is diabolic, and set up a cry of `over-population.' But your slaves are beyond caring for your cries: they breed like rabbits: and their poverty breeds filth, ugliness, dishonesty, disease, obscenity, drunkenness."

Lack of insight into fundamental truths of human nature is evident throughout the writings of the Marxians. The Marxian Socialists, according to Kautsky, defended women in industry: it was right for woman to work in factories in order to preserve her equality with man! Man must not support woman, declared the great French Socialist Guesde, because that would make her the *proletaire* of man! Bebel, the great authority on woman, famous for his erudition, having critically studied the problem of population, suggested as a remedy for too excessive fecundity the consumption of a certain lard soup

---

[29] Fabian Essays in Socialism. p. 21.

reputed to have an "anti-generative" effect upon the agricultural population of Upper Bavaria! Such are the results of the literal and uncritical acceptance of Marx's static and mechanical conception of human society, a society perfectly automatic; in which competition is always operating at maximum efficiency; one vast and unending conspiracy against the blameless proletariat.

This lack of insight of the orthodox Marxians, long represented by the German Social-Democrats, is nowhere better illustrated than in Dr. Robinson's account of a mass meeting of the Social-Democrat party to organize public opinion against the doctrine of Birth Control among the poor.[30] "Another meeting had taken place the week before, at which several eminent Socialist women, among them Rosa Luxemburg and Clara Zetkin, spoke very strongly against limitation of offspring among the poor—in fact the title of the discussion was *Gegen den Geburtstreik*! 'Against the birth strike!'" The interest of the audience was intense. One could see that with them it was not merely a dialectic question, as it was with their leaders, but a matter of life and death. I came to attend a meeting *against* the limitation of offspring; it soon proved to be a meeting very decidedly *for* the limitation of offspring, for every speaker who spoke in favor of the artificial prevention of conception or undesired pregnancies, was greeted with vociferous, long-lasting applause; while those who tried to persuade the people that a limited number of children is not a proletarian weapon, and would not improve their lot, were so hissed that they had difficulty going on. The speakers who were against the... idea soon felt that their audience was against them.... Why was there such small attendance at the regular Socialistic meetings, while the meetings of this character were packed to suffocation? It did not apparently penetrate the leaders' heads that the reason was a simple one. Those meetings were evidently of no interest to them, while those which dealt with the limitation of offspring were of personal, vital, present interest.... What particularly amused me—and pained me—in the anti-limitationists was the ease and equanimity with which they advised the poor women to keep on bearing children. The woman herself was not taken into consideration, as if she was not a human being, but a machine. What are her sufferings, her labor pains, her inability to read, to attend meetings, to have a taste of life? What does she amount to? The proletariat needs fighters. Go on, females, and breed like animals. Maybe of the thousands you bear a few will become party members...."

The militant organization of the Marxian Socialists suggests that their campaign must assume the tactics of militarism of the familiar type. As represented by militaristic governments, militarism like Socialism has always encouraged the proletariat to increase and multiply. Imperial Germany was the outstanding and awful example of this attitude. Before the war the fall in the birth-rate was viewed by the Junker party with the gravest misgivings.

---

[30] Uncontrolled Breeding, By Adelyne More. p. 84.

59

Bernhardi and the protagonists of *Deutschland-über-alles* condemned it in the strongest terms. The Marxians unconsciously repeat the words of the government representative, Krohne, who, in a debate on the subject in the Prussian Diet, February 1916, asserted: "Unfortunately this view has gained followers amongst the German women.... These women, in refusing to rear strong and able children to continue the race, drag into the dust that which is the highest end of women—motherhood. It is to be hoped that the willingness to bear sacrifices will lead to a change for the better.... We need an increase in human beings to guard against the attacks of envious neighbors as well as to fulfil our cultural mission. Our whole economic development depends on increase of our people." Today we are fully aware of how imperial Germany fulfilled that cultural mission of hers; nor can we overlook the fact that the countries with a smaller birth-rate survived the ordeal. Even from the traditional militaristic standpoint, strength does not reside in numbers, though the Caesars, the Napoleons and the Kaisers of the world have always believed that large exploitable populations were necessary for their own individual power. If Marxian dictatorship means the dictatorship of a small minority wielding power in the interest of the proletariat, a high-birth rate may be necessary, though we may here recall the answer of the lamented Dr. Alfred Fried to the German imperialists: "It is madness, the apotheosis of unreason, to wish to breed and care for human beings in order that in the flower of their youth they may be sent in millions to be slaughtered wholesale by machinery. We need no wholesale production of men, have no need of the `fruitful fertility of women,' no need of wholesale wares, fattened and dressed for slaughter What we do need is careful maintenance of those already born. If the bearing of children is a moral and religious duty, then it is a much higher duty to secure the sacredness and security of human life, so that children born and bred with trouble and sacrifice may not be offered up in the bloom of youth to a political dogma at the bidding of secret diplomacy."

Marxism has developed a patriotism of its own, if indeed it has not yet been completely crystallized into a religion. Like the "capitalistic" governments it so vehemently attacks, it demands self-sacrifice and even martyrdom from the faithful comrades. But since its strength depends to so great a degree upon "conversion," upon docile acceptance of the doctrines of the "Master" as interpreted by the popes and bishops of this new church, it fails to arouse the irreligious proletariat. The Marxian Socialist boasts of his understanding of "working class psychology" and criticizes the lack of this understanding on the part of all dissenters. But, as the Socialists' meetings against the "birth strike" indicate, the working class is not interested in such generalities as the Marxian "theory of value," the "iron law" of wages, "the value of commodities" and the rest of the hazy articles of faith. Marx inherited the rigid nationalistic psychology of the eighteenth century, and his followers, for the most part, have accepted his mechanical and superficial treatment of instinct.[31] Discontented workers may rally to Marxism because it places the blame for their misery outside of themselves and depicts their conditions as the result of a capitalistic conspiracy, thereby satisfying that innate tendency of every human being to shift the blame to some living person outside himself, and because it strengthens his belief that his sufferings and difficulties may be overcome by the immediate amelioration of his economic environment. In this manner, psychologists tell us, neuroses and inner compulsions are fostered. No true solution is possible, to continue this analogy, until the worker is awakened to the realization that the roots of his malady lie deep in his own nature, his own organism, his own habits. To blame everything upon the capitalist and the environment produced by capitalism is to focus attention upon merely one of the elements of the problem. The Marxian too often forgets that before there was a capitalist there was exercised the unlimited reproductive activity of mankind, which produced the first overcrowding, the first want. This goaded humanity into its industrial frenzy, into warfare and theft and slavery. Capitalism has not created the lamentable state of affairs in which the world now finds itself. It has grown out of them, armed with the inevitable power to take advantage of our swarming, spawning millions. As that valiant thinker Monsieur G. Hardy has pointed out[32] the proletariat may be looked upon, not as the antagonist of capitalism, but as its accomplice. Labor surplus, or the "army of reserve" which as for decades and centuries furnished the industrial background of human misery, which so invariably defeats strikes and labor revolts, cannot honestly be blamed upon capitalism. It is, as M. Hardy points out, of *sexual* and proletarian origin. In bringing too many children into the world, in adding to the total of misery, in intensifying the evils of overcrowding, the proletariat itself increases the burden of organized labor; even of the Socialist and Syndicalist organizations themselves with a surplus of the docilely inefficient, with those great uneducable and unorganizable masses. With surprisingly few exceptions, Marxians of all countries have docilely followed their master in rejecting, with bitterness and vindictiveness that is difficult to explain, the principles and teachings of Birth Control.

Hunger alone is not responsible for the bitter struggle for existence we witness to-day in our over-advertised civilization. Sex, uncontrolled, misdirected, over-stimulated and misunderstood, has run riot at the instigation of priest, militarist and exploiter. Uncontrolled sex has rendered the proletariat prostrate, the capitalist powerful. In this continuous, unceasing alliance of sexual instinct and hunger we find the reason for the decline of all the finer sentiments. These instincts tear asunder the thin veils of culture and hypocrisy and expose to our gaze the dark sufferings of gaunt humanity. So

---

[31] For a sympathetic treatment of modern psychological research as bearing on Communism, by two convinced Communists see "Creative Revolution," by Eden and Cedar Paul.

[32] Neo-Malthusianisme et Socialisme, p. 22.

have we become familiar with the everyday spectacle of distorted bodies, of harsh and frightful diseases stalking abroad in the light of day; of misshapen heads and visages of moron and imbecile; of starving children in city streets and schools. This is the true soil of unspeakable crimes. Defect and delinquency join hands with disease, and accounts of inconceivable and revolting vices are dished up in the daily press. When the majority of men and women are driven by the grim lash of sex and hunger in the unending struggle to feed themselves and to carry the dead-weight of dead and dying progeny, when little children are forced into factories, streets, and shops, education—including even education in the Marxian dogmas—is quite impossible; and civilization is more completely threatened than it ever could be by pestilence or war.

But, it will be pointed out, the working class has advanced. Power has been acquired by labor unions and syndicates. In the beginning power was won by the principle of the restriction of numbers. The device of refusing to admit more than a fixed number of new members to the unions of the various trades has been justified as necessary for the upholding of the standard of wages and of working conditions. This has been the practice in precisely those unions which have been able through years of growth and development to attain tangible strength and power. Such a principle of restriction is necessary in the creation of a firmly and deeply rooted trunk or central organization furnishing a local center for more extended organization. It is upon this great principle of restricted number that the labor unions have generated and developed power. They have acquired this power without any religious emotionalism, without subscribing to metaphysical or economic theology. For the millenium and the earthly paradise to be enjoyed at some indefinitely future date, the union member substitutes the very real politics of organization with its resultant benefits. He increases his own independence and comfort and that of his family. He is immune to superstitious belief in and respect for the mysterious power of political or economic nostrums to reconstruct human society according to the Marxian formula.

In rejecting the Marxian hypothesis as superficial and fragmentary, we do so not because of its so-called revolutionary character, its threat to the existing order of things, but rather because of its superficial, emotional and religious character and its deleterious effect upon the life of reason. Like other schemes advanced by the alarmed and the indignant, it relies too much upon moral fervor and enthusiasm. To build any social program upon the shifting sands of sentiment and feeling, of indignation or enthusiasm, is a dangerous and foolish task. On the other hand, we should not minimize the importance of the Socialist movement in so valiantly and so courageously battling against the stagnating complacency of our conservatives and reactionaries, under whose benign imbecility the defective and diseased elements of humanity are encouraged "full speed ahead" in their reckless and irresponsible swarming and spawning. Nevertheless, as George Drysdale pointed out nearly seventy years ago;

"... If we ignore this and other sexual subjects, we may do whatever else we like: we may bully, we may bluster, we may rage, We may foam at the mouth; we may tear down Heaven with our prayers, we may exhaust ourselves with weeping over the sorrows of the poor; we may narcotize ourselves and others with the opiate of Christian resignation; we may dissolve the realities of human woe in a delusive mirage of poetry and ideal philosophy; we may lavish our substance in charity, and labor over possible or impossible Poor Laws; we may form wild dreams of Socialism, industrial regiments, universal brotherhood, red republics, or unexampled revolutions; we may strangle and murder each other, we may persecute and despise those whose sexual necessities force them to break through our unnatural moral codes; we may burn alive if we please the prostitutes and the adulterers; we may break our own and our neighbor's hearts against the adamantine laws that surround us, but not one step, not one shall we advance, till we acknowledge these laws, and adopt the only possible mode in which they can be obeyed." These words were written in 1854. Recent events have accentuated their stinging truth.

CHAPTER VIII: Dangers of Cradle Competition

Eugenics has been defined as "the study of agencies under social control that may improve or impair the racial qualities of future generations, either mentally or physically." While there is no inherent conflict between Socialism and Eugenics, the latter is, broadly, the antithesis of the former. In its propaganda, Socialism emphasizes the evil effects of our industrial and economic system. It insists upon the necessity of satisfying material needs, upon sanitation, hygiene, and education to effect the transformation of society. The Socialist insists that healthy humanity is impossible without a radical improvement of the social—and therefore of the economic and industrial—environment. The Eugenist points out that heredity is the great determining factor in the lives of men and women. Eugenics is the attempt to solve the problem from the biological and evolutionary point of view. You may bring all the changes possible on "Nurture" or environment, the Eugenist may say to the Socialist, but comparatively little can be effected until you control biological and hereditary elements of the problem. Eugenics thus aims to seek out the root of our trouble, to study humanity as a kinetic, dynamic, evolutionary organism, shifting and changing with the successive generations, rising and falling, cleansing itself of inherent defects, or under adverse and dysgenic influences, sinking into degeneration and deterioration.

"Eugenics" was first defined by Sir Francis Galton in his "Human Faculty" in 1884, and was subsequently developed into a science and into an educational effort. Galton's ideal was the rational breeding of human beings. The aim of Eugenics, as defined by its founder, is to bring as many influences as can be reasonably employed, to cause the useful classes of the community to contribute *more* than their proportion to the next generation. Eugenics thus concerns itself with all influences that improve the inborn qualities of a race; also with those that develop them to the utmost advantage. It is, in short, the attempt to bring reason and intelligence to bear upon *heredity*. But Galton, in spite of the immense value of this approach and his great stimulation to criticism, was completely unable to formulate a definite and practical working program. He hoped at length to introduce Eugenics "into the national conscience like a new religion.... I see no impossibility in Eugenics becoming a religious dogma among mankind, but its details must first be worked out sedulously in the study. Over-zeal leading to hasty action, would do harm by holding out expectations of a new golden age, which will certainly be falsified and cause the science to be discredited. The first and main point is to secure the general intellectual acceptance of Eugenics as a hopeful and most important study. Then, let its principles work into the heart of the nation, who will gradually give practical effect to them in ways that we may not wholly foresee."[33]

Galton formulated a general law of inheritance which declared that an individual receives one-half of his inheritance from his two parents, one-fourth from his four grandparents, one-eighth from his great-grandparents, one-sixteenth from his great-great grandparents, and so on by diminishing fractions to his primordial ancestors, the sum of all these fractions added together contributing to the whole of the inherited make-up. The trouble with this generalization, from the modern Mendelian point of view, is that it fails to define what "characters" one would get in the one-half that came from one's parents, or the one-fourth from one's grandparents. The whole of our inheritance is not composed of these indefinitely made up fractional parts. We are interested rather in those more specific traits or characters, mental or physical, which, in the Mendelian view, are structural and functional units, making up a mosaic rather than a blend. The laws of heredity are concerned with the precise behavior, during a series of generations, of these specific unit characters. This behavior, as the study of Genetics shows, may be determined in lesser organisms by experiment. Once determined, they are subject to prophecy.

The problem of human heredity is now seen to be infinitely more complex than imagined by Galton and his followers, and the optimistic hope of elevating Eugenics to the level of a religion is a futile one. Most of the Eugenists, including Professor Karl Pearson and his colleagues of the Eugenics Laboratory of the University of London and of the biometric laboratory in University College, have retained the age-old point of view of "Nature vs. Nurture" and have attempted to show the predominating influence of Heredity *as opposed to* Environment. This may be true; but demonstrated and repeated in investigation after investigation, it nevertheless remains fruitless and unprofitable from the practical point of view.

We should not minimize the great outstanding service of Eugenics for critical and diagnostic investigations. It demonstrates, not in terms of glittering generalization but in statistical studies of investigations reduced to measurement and number, that uncontrolled fertility is universally correlated with disease, poverty, overcrowding and the transmission of hereditable taints. Professor Pearson and his associates show us that "if fertility be correlated with anti-social hereditary characters, a population will inevitably degenerate."

This degeneration has already begun. Eugenists demonstrate that two-thirds of our manhood of military age are physically too unfit to shoulder a rifle; that the feeble-minded, the syphilitic, the irresponsible and the defective breed unhindered; that women are driven into factories and shops on day-shift and night-shift; that children, frail carriers of the torch of life, are put to work

---

[33] Galton. Essays in Eugenics, p. 43.

at an early age; that society at large is breeding an ever-increasing army of under-sized, stunted and dehumanized slaves; that the vicious circle of mental and physical defect, delinquency and beggary is encouraged, by the unseeing and unthinking sentimentality of our age, to populate asylum, hospital and prison.

All these things the Eugenists sees and points out with a courage entirely admirable. But as a positive program of redemption, orthodox Eugenics can offer nothing more "constructive" than a renewed "cradle competition" between the "fit" and the "unfit." It sees that the most responsible and most intelligent members of society are the less fertile; that the feeble-minded are the more fertile. Herein lies the unbalance, the great biological menace to the future of civilization. Are we heading to biological destruction, toward the gradual but certain attack upon the stocks of intelligence and racial health by the sinister forces of the hordes of irresponsibility and imbecility? This is not such a remote danger as the optimistic Eugenist might suppose. The mating of the moron with a person of sound stock may, as Dr. Tredgold points out, gradually disseminate this trait far and wide until it undermines the vigor and efficiency of an entire nation and an entire race. This is no idle fancy. We must take it into account if we wish to escape the fate that has befallen so many civilizations in the past.

"It is, indeed, more than likely that the presence of this impairment in a mitigated form is responsible for no little of the defective character, the diminution of mental and moral fiber at the present day," states Dr. Tredgold.[34] Such populations, this distinguished authority might have added, form the veritable "cultures" not only for contagious physical diseases but for mental instability and irresponsibility also. They are susceptible, exploitable, hysterical, non-resistant to external suggestion. Devoid of stamina, such folk become mere units in a mob. "The habit of crowd-making is daily becoming a more serious menace to civilization," writes Everett Dean Martin. "Our society is becoming a veritable babel of gibbering crowds."[35] It would be only the incorrigible optimist who refused to see the integral relation between this phenomenon and the indiscriminate breeding by which we recruit our large populations.

The danger of recruiting our numbers from the most "fertile stocks" is further emphasized when we recall that in a democracy like that of the United States every man and woman is permitted a vote in the government, and that it is the representatives of this grade of intelligence who may destroy our liberties, and who may thus be the most far-reaching peril to the future of civilization.

"It is a pathological worship of mere number," writes Alleyne Ireland, "which has inspired all the efforts—the primary, the direct election of

---

[34] Eugenics Review, Vol. XIII, p. 349.
[35] Cf. Martin, The Behavior of Crowds, p. 6.

Senators, the initiative, the recall and the referendum—to cure the evils of mob rule by increasing the size of the mob and extending its powers."[36]

Equality of political power has thus been bestowed upon the lowest elements of our population. We must not be surprised, therefore, at the spectacle of political scandal and graft, of the notorious and universally ridiculed low level of intelligence and flagrant stupidity exhibited by our legislative bodies. The Congressional Record mirrors our political imbecility.

All of these dangers and menaces are acutely realized by the Eugenists; it is to them that we are most indebted for the proof that reckless spawning carries with it the seeds of destruction. But whereas the Galtonians reveal themselves as unflinching in their investigation and in their exhibition of fact and diagnoses of symptoms, they do not on the other hand show much power in suggesting practical and feasible remedies.

On its scientific side, Eugenics suggests the reestabilishment of the balance between the fertility of the "fit" and the "unfit." The birth-rate among the normal and healthier and finer stocks of humanity, is to be increased by awakening among the "fit" the realization of the dangers of a lessened birth-rate in proportion to the reckless breeding among the "unfit." By education, by persuasion, by appeals to racial ethics and religious motives, the ardent Eugenist hopes to increase the fertility of the "fit." Professor Pearson thinks that it is especially necessary to awaken the hardiest stocks to this duty. These stocks, he says, are to be found chiefly among the skilled artisan class, the intelligent working class. Here is a fine combination of health and hardy vigor, of sound body and sound mind.

Professor Pearson and his school of biometrics here ignore or at least fail to record one of those significant "correlations" which form the basis of his method. The publications of the Eugenics Laboratory all tend to show that a high rate of fertility is correlated with extreme poverty, recklessness, deficiency and delinquency; similarly, that among the more intelligent, this rate of fertility decreases. But the scientific Eugenists fail to recognize that this restraint of fecundity is due to a deliberate foresight and is a conscious effort to elevate standards of living for the family and the children of the responsible—and possibly more selfish—sections of the community. The appeal to enter again into competitive child-bearing, for the benefit of the nation or the race, or any other abstraction, will fall on deaf ears.

Pearson has done invaluable work in pointing out the fallacies and the false conclusions of the ordinary statisticians. But when he attempts to show by the methods of biometrics that not only the first child but also the second, are especially liable to suffer from transmissible pathological defects, such as insanity, criminality and tuberculosis, he fails to recognize that this tendency is counterbalanced by the high mortality rate among later children. If first and second children reveal a greater percentage of heritable defect, it is because

---

[36] Cf. Democracy and the Human Equation. E. P. Dutton & Co., 1921.

67

the later born children are less liable to survive the conditions produced by a large family.

In passing, we should here recognize the difficulties presented by the idea of "fit" and "unfit." Who is to decide this question? The grosser, the more obvious, the undeniably feeble-minded should, indeed, not only be discouraged but prevented from propagating their kind. But among the writings of the representative Eugenists one cannot ignore the distinct middle-class bias that prevails. As that penetrating critic, F. W. Stella Browne, has said in another connection, "The Eugenics Education Society has among its numbers many most open-minded and truly progressive individuals but the official policy it has pursued for years has been inspired by class-bias and sex bias. The society laments with increasing vehemence the multiplication of the less fortunate classes at a more rapid rate than the possessors of leisure and opportunity. (I do not think it relevant here to discuss whether the innate superiority of endowment in the governing class really is so overwhelming as to justify the Eugenics Education Society's peculiar use of the terms `fit' and `unfit'!) Yet it has persistently refused to give any help toward extending the knowledge of contraceptives to the exploited classes. Similarly, though the Eugenics Review, the organ of the society, frequently laments the `selfishness' of the refusal of maternity by healthy and educated women of the professional classes, I have yet to learn that it has made any official pronouncement on the English illegitimacy laws or any organized effort toward defending the unmarried mother."

This peculiarly Victorian reticence may be inherited from the founder of Eugenics. Galton declared that the "Bohemian" element in the Anglo-Saxon race is destined to perish, and "the sooner it goes, the happier for mankind." The trouble with any effort of trying to divide humanity into the "fit" and the "unfit," is that we do not want, as H. G. Wells recently pointed out,[37] to breed for uniformity but for variety. "We want statesmen and poets and musicians and philosophers and strong men and delicate men and brave men. The qualities of one would be the weaknesses of the other." We want, most of all, genius.

Proscription on Galtonian lines would tend to eliminate many of the great geniuses of the world who were not only "Bohemian," but actually and pathologically abnormal—men like Rousseau, Dostoevsky, Chopin, Poe, Schumann, Nietzsche, Comte, Guy de Maupassant,—and how many others? But such considerations should not lead us into error of concluding that such men were geniuses merely because they were pathological specimens, and that the only way to produce a genius is to breed disease and defect. It only emphasizes the dangers of external standards of "fit" and "unfit."

These limitations are more strikingly shown in the types of so-called "eugenic" legislation passed or proposed by certain enthusiasts. Regulation,

---

[37] Cf. The Salvaging of Civilization.

compulsion and prohibitions affected and enacted by political bodies are the surest methods of driving the whole problem under-ground. As Havelock Ellis has pointed out, the absurdity and even hopelessness of effecting Eugenic improvement by placing on the statute books prohibitions of legal matrimony to certain classes of people, reveal the weakness of those Eugenists who minimize or undervalue the importance of environment as a determining factor. They affirm that heredity is everything and environment nothing, yet forget that it is precisely those who are most universally subject to bad environment who procreate most copiously, most recklessly and most disastrously. Such marriage laws are based for the most part on the infantile assumption that procreation is absolutely dependent upon the marriage ceremony, an assumption usually coupled with the complementary one that the only purpose in marriage is procreation. Yet it is a fact so obvious that it is hardly worth stating that the most fertile classes who indulge in the most dysgenic type of procreating—the feeble-minded—are almost totally unaffected by marriage laws and marriage-ceremonies.

As for the sterilization of habitual criminals, not merely must we know more of heredity and genetics in general, but also acquire more certainty of the justice of our laws and the honesty of their administration before we can make rulings of fitness or unfitness merely upon the basis of a respect for law. On this point the eminent William Bateson writes:[38] "Criminals are often feeble-minded, but as regards those that are not, the fact that a man is for the purposes of Society classified as a criminal, tells me little as to his value, still less as to the possible value of his offspring. It is a fault inherent in criminal jurisprudence, based on non-biological data, that the law must needs take the nature of the offenses rather than that of the offenders as the basis of classification. A change in the right direction has begun, but the problem is difficult and progress will be very slow.... We all know of persons convicted, perhaps even habitually, whom the world could ill spare. Therefore I hesitate to proscribe the criminal. Proscription... is a weapon with a very nasty recoil. Might not some with equal cogency proscribe army contractors and their accomplices, the newspaper patriots? The crimes of the prison population are petty offenses by comparison, and the significance we attach to them is a survival of other days. Felonies may be great events, locally, but they do not induce catastrophies. The proclivities of the war-makers are infinitely more dangerous than those of the aberrant beings whom from time to time the law may dub as criminal. Consistent and portentous selfishness, combined with dullness of imagination is probably just as transmissible as want of self-control, though destitute of the amiable qualities not rarely associated with the genetic composition of persons of unstable mind."

In this connection, we should note another type of "respectable" criminality noted by Havelock Ellis: "If those persons who raise the cry of

---

[38] Common Sense in Racial Problems. By W. Bateson, M. A. A., F. R. S.

'race-suicide' in face of the decline of the birth-rate really had the knowledge and the intelligence to realize the manifold evils which they are invoking, they would deserve to be treated as criminals."

Our debt to the science of Eugenics is great in that it directs our attention to the biological nature of humanity. Yet there is too great a tendency among the thinkers of this school, to restrict their ideas of sex to its expression as a purely procreative function. Compulsory legislation which would make the inevitably futile attempt to prohibit one of the most beneficent and necessary of human expressions, or regulate it into the channels of preconceived philosophies, would reduce us to the unpleasant days predicted by William Blake, when

> *"Priests in black gowns will be walking their rounds And binding with briars our joys and desires."*

Eugenics is chiefly valuable in its negative aspects. It is "negative Eugenics" that has studied the histories of such families as the Jukeses and the Kallikaks, that has pointed out the network of imbecility and feeble-mindedness that has been sedulously spread through all strata of society. On its so-called positive or constructive side, it fails to awaken any permanent interest. "Constructive" Eugenics aims to arouse the enthusiasm or the interest of the people in the welfare of the world fifteen or twenty generations in the future. On its negative side it shows us that we are paying for and even submitting to the dictates of an ever increasing, unceasingly spawning class of human beings who never should have been born at all—that the wealth of individuals and of states is being diverted from the development and the progress of human expression and civilization.

While it is necessary to point out the importance of "heredity" as a determining factor in human life, it is fatal to elevate it to the position of an absolute. As with environment, the concept of heredity derives its value and its meaning only in so far as it is embodied and made concrete in generations of living organisms. Environment and heredity are not antagonistic. Our problem is not that of "Nature vs. Nurture," but rather of Nature X Nurture, of heredity multiplied by environment, if we may express it thus. The Eugenist who overlooks the importance of environment as a determining factor in human life, is as short-sighted as the Socialist who neglects the biological nature of man. We cannot disentangle these two forces, except in theory. To the child in the womb, said Samuel Butler, the mother is "environment." She is, of course, likewise "heredity." The age-old discussion of "Nature vs. Nurture" has been threshed out time after time, usually fruitlessly, because of a failure to recognize the indivisibility of these biological factors. The opposition or antagonism between them is an artificial and academic one, having no basis in the living organism.

The great principle of Birth Control offers the means whereby the individual may adapt himself to and even control the forces of environment and heredity. Entirely apart from its Malthusian aspect or that of the population question, Birth Control must be recognized, as the Neo-Malthusians pointed out long ago, not "merely as the key of the social position," and the only possible and practical method of human generation, but as the very pivot of civilization. Birth Control which has been criticized as negative and destructive, is really the greatest and most truly eugenic method, and its adoption as part of the program of Eugenics would immediately give a concrete and realistic power to that science. As a matter of fact, Birth Control has been accepted by the most clear thinking and far seeing of the Eugenists themselves as the most constructive and necessary of the means to racial health.[39]

---

[39] Among these are Dean W. R. Inge, Professor J. Arthur Thomson, Dr. Havelock Ellis, Professor William Bateson, Major Leonard Darwin and Miss Norah March.

CHAPTER IX: A Moral Necessity

I went to the Garden of Love,
And saw what I never had seen;
A Chapel was built in the midst,
Where I used to play on the green.

And the gates of this Chapel were shut,
And "Thou shalt not" writ over the door;
So I turned to the Garden of Love
That so many sweet flowers bore.

And I saw it was filled with graves,
And tombstones where flowers should be;
And priests in black gowns were walking their rounds,
And binding with briars my joys and desires.

—William Blake

Orthodox opposition to Birth Control is formulated in the official protest of the National Council of Catholic Women against the resolution passed by the New York State Federation of Women's Clubs which favored the removal of all obstacles to the spread of information regarding practical methods of Birth Control. The Catholic statement completely embodies traditional opposition to Birth Control. It affords a striking contrast by which we may clarify and justify the ethical necessity for this new instrument of civilization as the most effective basis for practical and scientific morality. "The authorities at Rome have again and again declared that all positive methods of this nature are immoral and forbidden," states the National Council of Catholic Women. "There is no question of the lawfulness of birth restriction through abstinence from the relations which result in conception. The immorality of Birth Control as it is practised and commonly understood, consists in the evils of the particular method employed. These are all contrary to the moral law because they are unnatural, being a perversion of a natural function. Human faculties are used in such a way as to frustrate the natural end for which these faculties were created. This is always intrinsically wrong—as wrong as lying and blasphemy. No supposed beneficial consequence can make good a practice which is, in itself, immoral....

"The evil results of the practice of Birth Control are numerous. Attention will be called here to only three. The first is the degradation of the marital relation itself, since the husband and wife who indulge in any form of this practice come to have a lower idea of married life. They cannot help coming to regard each other to a great extent as mutual instruments of sensual gratification, rather than as cooperators with the Creating in bringing children into the world. This consideration may be subtle but it undoubtedly represents the facts.

"In the second place, the deliberate restriction of the family through these immoral practices deliberately weakens self-control and the capacity for self-denial, and increases the love of ease and luxury. The best indication of this is that the small family is much more prevalent in the classes that are comfortable and well-to-do than among those whose material advantages are moderate or small. The theory of the advocates of Birth Control is that those parents who are comfortably situated should have a large number of children (sic!) while the poor should restrict their offspring to a much smaller number. This theory does not work, for the reason that each married couple have their own idea of what constitutes unreasonable hardship in the matter of bearing and rearing children. A large proportion of the parents who are addicted to Birth Control practices are sufficiently provided with worldly goods to be free from apprehension on the economic side; nevertheless, they have small families because they are disinclined to undertake the other burdens involved in bringing up a more numerous family. A practice which tends to produce such exaggerated notions of what constitutes hardship, which leads men and women to cherish such a degree of ease, makes inevitably for inefficiency, a decline in the capacity to endure and to achieve, and for a general social decadence.

"Finally, Birth Control leads sooner or later to a decline in population...." (The case of France is instanced.) But it is essentially the moral question that alarms the Catholic women, for the statement concludes: "The further effect of such proposed legislation will inevitably be a lowering both of public and private morals. What the fathers of this country termed indecent and forbade the mails to carry, will, if such legislation is carried through, be legally decent. The purveyors of sexual license and immorality will have the opportunity to send almost anything they care to write through the mails on the plea that it is sex information. Not only the married but also the unmarried will be thus affected; the ideals of the young contaminated and lowered. The morals of the entire nation will suffer.

"The proper attitude of Catholics... is clear. They should watch and oppose all attempts in state legislatures and in Congress to repeal the laws which now prohibit the dissemination of information concerning Birth Control. Such information will be spread only too rapidly despite existing laws. To repeal these would greatly accelerate this deplorable movement."[40]

The Catholic position has been stated in an even more extreme form by Archbishop Patrick J. Hayes of the archdiocese of New York. In a "Christmas Pastoral" this dignitary even went to the extent of declaring that "even though some little angels in the flesh, through the physical or mental deformities of

---

[40] Quoted in the National Catholic Welfare Council Bulletin: Vol. II, No. 5, p. 21 (January, 1921).

their parents, may appear to human eyes hideous, misshapen, a blot on civilized society, we must not lose sight of this Christian thought that under and within such visible malformation, lives an immortal soul to be saved and glorified for all eternity among the blessed in heaven."[41]

With the type of moral philosophy expressed in this utterance, we need not argue. It is based upon traditional ideas that have had the practical effect of making this world a vale of tears. Fortunately such words carry no weight with those who can bring free and keen as well as noble minds to the consideration of the matter. To them the idealism of such an utterance appears crude and cruel. The menace to civilization of such orthodoxy, if it be orthodoxy, lies in the fact that its powerful exponents may be for a time successful not merely in influencing the conduct of their adherents but in checking freedom of thought and discussion. To this, with all the vehemence of emphasis at our command, we object. From what Archbishop Hayes believes concerning the future blessedness in Heaven of the souls of those who are born into this world as hideous and misshapen beings he has a right to seek such consolation as may be obtained; but we who are trying to better the conditions of this world believe that a healthy, happy human race is more in keeping with the laws of God, than disease, misery and poverty perpetuating itself generation after generation. Furthermore, while conceding to Catholic or other churchmen full freedom to preach their own doctrines, whether of theology or morals, nevertheless when they attempt to carry these ideas into legislative acts and force their opinions and codes upon the non-Catholics, we consider such action an interference with the principles of democracy and we have a right to protest.

Religious propaganda against Birth Control is crammed with contradiction and fallacy. It refutes itself. Yet it brings the opposing views into vivid contrast. In stating these differences we should make clear that advocates of Birth Control are not seeking to attack the Catholic church. We quarrel with that church, however, when it seeks to assume authority over non-Catholics and to dub their behavior immoral because they do not conform to the dictatorship of Rome. The question of bearing and rearing children we hold is the concern of the mother and the potential mother. If she delegates the responsibility, the ethical education, to an external authority, that is her affair. We object, however, to the State or the Church which appoints itself as arbiter and dictator in this sphere and attempts to force unwilling women into compulsory maternity.

When Catholics declare that "The authorities at Rome have again and again declared that all positive methods of this nature are immoral and forbidden," they do so upon the assumption that morality consists in conforming to laws laid down and enforced by external authority, in submission to decrees and dicta imposed from without. In this case, they

---

[41] Quoted in daily press, December 19, 1921.

decide in a wholesale manner the conduct of millions, demanding of them not the intelligent exercise of their own individual judgment and discrimination, but unquestioning submission and conformity to dogma. The Church thus takes the place of all-powerful parents, and demands of its children merely that they should obey. In my belief such a philosophy hampers the development of individual intelligence. Morality then becomes a more or less successful attempt to conform to a code, instead of an attempt to bring reason and intelligence to bear upon the solution of each individual human problem.

But, we read on, Birth Control methods are not merely contrary to "moral law," but forbidden because they are "unnatural," being "the perversion of a natural function." This, of course, is the weakest link in the whole chain. Yet "there is no question of the lawfulness of birth restriction through abstinence"—as though abstinence itself were not unnatural! For more than a thousand years the Church was occupied with the problem of imposing abstinence on its priesthood, its most educated and trained body of men, educated to look upon asceticism as the finest ideal; it took one thousand years to convince the Catholic priesthood that abstinence was "natural" or practicable.[42] Nevertheless, there is still this talk of abstinence, self-control, and self-denial, almost in the same breath with the condemnation of Birth Control as "unnatural."

If it is our duty to act as "cooperators with the Creator" to bring children into the world, it is difficult to say at what point our behavior is "unnatural." If it is immoral and "unnatural" to prevent an unwanted life from coming into existence, is it not immoral and "unnatural" to remain unmarried from the age of puberty? Such casuistry is unconvincing and feeble. We need only point out that rational intelligence is also a "natural" function, and that it is as imperative for us to use the faculties of judgment, criticism, discrimination of choice, selection and control, all the faculties of the intelligence, as it is to use those of reproduction. It is certainly dangerous "to frustrate the natural ends for which these faculties were created." This also, is always intrinsically wrong—as wrong as lying and blasphemy—and infinitely more devastating. Intelligence is as natural to us as any other faculty, and it is fatal to moral development and growth to refuse to use it and to delegate to others the solution of our individual problems. The evil will not be that one's conduct is divergent from current and conventional moral codes. There may be every outward evidence of conformity, but this agreement may be arrived at, by the restriction and suppression of subjective desires, and the more or less successful attempt at mere conformity. Such "morality" would conceal an inner conflict. The fruits of this conflict would be neurosis and hysteria on the one hand; or concealed gratification of suppressed desires on the other, with a resultant hypocrisy and cant. True morality cannot be based on conformity. There must be no conflict between subjective desire and outward behavior.

---

[42] H. C. Lea: History of Sacerdotal Celibacy (Philadelphia, 1867).

To object to these traditional and churchly ideas does not by any means imply that the doctrine of Birth Control is anti-Christian. On the contrary, it may be profoundly in accordance with the Sermon on the Mount. One of the greatest living theologians and most penetrating students of the problems of civilization is of this opinion. In an address delivered before the Eugenics Education Society of London,[43] William Ralph Inge, the Very Reverend Dean of St. Paul's Cathedral, London, pointed out that the doctrine of Birth Control was to be interpreted as of the very essence of Christianity.

"We should be ready to give up all our theories," he asserted, "if science proved that we were on the wrong lines. And we can understand, though we profoundly disagree with, those who oppose us on the grounds of authority.... We know where we are with a man who says, `Birth Control is forbidden by God; we prefer poverty, unemployment, war, the physical, intellectual and moral degeneration of the people, and a high death rate, to any interference with the universal command to be fruitful and multiply'; but we have no patience with those who say that we can have unrestricted and unregulated propagation without those consequences. It is a great part of our work to press home to the public mind the alternative that lies before us. Either rational selection must take the place of the natural selection which the modern State will not allow to act, or we must go on deteriorating. When we can convince the public of this, the opposition of organized religion will soon collapse or become ineffective." Dean Inge effectively answers those who have objected to the methods of Birth Control as "immoral" and in contradiction and inimical to the teachings of Christ. Incidentally he claims that those who are not blinded by prejudices recognize that "Christianity aims at saving the soul—the personality, the nature, of man, not his body or his environment. According to Christianity, a man is saved, not by what he has, or knows, or does, but by what he is. It treats all the apparatus of life with a disdain as great as that of the biologist; so long as a man is inwardly healthy, it cares very little whether he is rich or poor, learned or simple, and even whether he is happy, or unhappy. It attaches no importance to quantitative measurements of any kind. The Christian does not gloat over favorable trade-statistics, nor congratulate himself on the disparity between the number of births and deaths. For him... the test of the welfare of a country is the quality of human beings whom it produces. Quality is everything, quantity is nothing. And besides this, the Christian conception of a kingdom of God upon the earth teaches us to turn our eyes to the future, and to think of the welfare of posterity as a thing which concerns us as much as that of our own generation. This welfare, as conceived by Christianity, is of course something different from external prosperity; it is to be the victory of intrinsic worth and healthiness over all the false ideals and deep-seated diseases which at present spoil civilization."

---

[43] Eugenics Review, January 1921.

"It is not political religion with which I am concerned," Dean Inge explained, "but the convictions of really religious persons; and I do not think that we need despair of converting them to our views."

Dean Inge believes Birth Control is an essential part of Eugenics, and an essential part of Christian morality. On this point he asserts: "We do wish to remind our orthodox and conservative friends that the Sermon on the Mount contains some admirably clear and unmistakable eugenic precepts. `Do men gather grapes of thorns, or figs of thistles? A corrupt tree cannot bring forth good fruit, neither can a good tree bring forth evil fruit. Every tree which bringeth not forth good fruit is hewn down, and cast into the fire.' We wish to apply these words not only to the actions of individuals, which spring from their characters, but to the character of individuals, which spring from their inherited qualities. This extension of the scope of the maxim seems to me quite legitimate. Men do not gather grapes of thorns. As our proverb says, you cannot make a silk purse out of a sow's ear. If we believe this, and do not act upon it by trying to move public opinion towards giving social reform, education and religion a better material to work upon, we are sinning against the light, and not doing our best to bring in the Kingdom of God upon earth."

As long as sexual activity is regarded in a dualistic and contradictory light,—in which it is revealed either as the instrument by which men and women "cooperate with the Creator" to bring children into the world, on the one hand; and on the other, as the sinful instrument of self-gratification, lust and sensuality, there is bound to be an endless conflict in human conduct, producing ever increasing misery, pain and injustice. In crystallizing and codifying this contradiction, the Church not only solidified its own power over men but reduced women to the most abject and prostrate slavery. It was essentially a morality that would not "work." The sex instinct in the human race is too strong to be bound by the dictates of any church. The church's failure, its century after century of failure, is now evident on every side: for, having convinced men and women that only in its baldly propagative phase is sexual expression legitimate, the teachings of the Church have driven sex under-ground, into secret channels, strengthened the conspiracy of silence, concentrated men's thoughts upon the "lusts of the body," have sown, cultivated and reaped a crop of bodily and mental diseases, and developed a society congenitally and almost hopelessly unbalanced. How is any progress to be made, how is any human expression or education possible when women and men are taught to combat and resist their natural impulses and to despise their bodily functions?

Humanity, we are glad to realize, is rapidly freeing itself from this "morality" imposed upon it by its self-appointed and self-perpetuating masters. From a hundred different points the imposing edifice of this "morality" has been and is being attacked. Sincere and thoughtful defenders and exponents of the teachings of Christ now acknowledge the falsity of the traditional codes and their malignant influence upon the moral and physical well-being of humanity.

Ecclesiastical opposition to Birth Control on the part of certain representatives of the Protestant churches, based usually on quotations from the Bible, is equally invalid, and for the same reason. The attitude of the more intelligent and enlightened clergy has been well and succinctly expressed by Dean Inge, who, referring to the ethics of Birth Control, writes: *"This is emphatically a matter in which every man and woman must judge for themselves, and must refrain from judging others."* We must not neglect the important fact that it is not merely in the practical results of such a decision, not in the small number of children, not even in the healthier and better cared for children, not in the possibility of elevating the living conditions of the individual family, that the ethical value of Birth Control alone lies. Precisely because the practice of Birth Control does demand the exercise of decision, the making of choice, the use of the reasoning powers, is it an instrument of moral education as well as of hygienic and racial advance. It awakens the attention of parents to their potential children. It forces upon the individual consciousness the question of the standards of living. In a profound manner it protects and reasserts the inalienable rights of the child-to-be.

Psychology and the outlook of modern life are stressing the growth of independent responsibility and discrimination as the true basis of ethics. The old traditional morality, with its train of vice, disease, promiscuity and prostitution, is in reality dying out, killing itself off because it is too irresponsible and too dangerous to individual and social well-being. The transition from the old to the new, like all fundamental changes, is fraught with many dangers. But it is a revolution that cannot be stopped.

The smaller family, with its lower infant mortality rate, is, in more definite and concrete manner than many actions outwardly deemed "moral," the expression of moral judgment and responsibility. It is the assertion of a standard of living, inspired by the wish to obtain a fuller and more expressive life for the children than the parents have enjoyed. If the morality or immorality of any course of conduct is to be determined by the motives which inspire it, there is evidently at the present day no higher morality than the intelligent practice of Birth Control.

The immorality of many who practise Birth Control lies in not daring to preach what they practise. What is the secret of the hypocrisy of the well-to-do, who are willing to contribute generously to charities and philanthropies, who spend thousands annually in the upkeep and sustenance of the delinquent, the defective and the dependent; and yet join the conspiracy of silence that prevents the poorer classes from learning how to improve their conditions, and elevate their standards of living? It is as though they were to cry: "We'll give you anything except the thing you ask for—the means whereby you may become responsible and self-reliant in your own lives."

The brunt of this injustice falls on women, because the old traditional morality is the invention of men. "No religion, no physical or moral code," wrote the clear-sighted George Drysdale, "proposed by one sex for the other, can be really suitable. Each must work out its laws for itself in every department of life." In the moral code developed by the Church, women have been so degraded that they have been habituated to look upon themselves through the eyes of men. Very imperfectly have women developed their own self-consciousness, the realization of their tremendous and supreme position in civilization. Women can develop this power only in one way; by the exercise of responsibility, by the exercise of judgment, reason or discrimination. They need ask for no "rights." They need only assert power. Only by the exercise of self-guidance and intelligent self-direction can that inalienable, supreme, pivotal power be expressed. More than ever in history women need to realize that nothing can ever come to us from another. Everything we attain we must owe to ourselves. Our own spirit must vitalize it. Our own heart must feel it. For we are not passive machines. We are not to be lectured, guided and molded this way or that. We are alive and intelligent, we women, no less than men, and we must awaken to the essential realization that we are living beings, endowed with will, choice, comprehension, and that every step in life must be taken at our own initiative.

Moral and sexual balance in civilization will only be established by the assertion and expression of power on the part of women. This power will not be found in any futile seeking for economic independence or in the aping of men in industrial and business pursuits, nor by joining battle for the so-called "single standard." Woman's power can only be expressed and make itself felt when she refuses the task of bringing unwanted children into the world to be exploited in industry and slaughtered in wars. When we refuse to produce battalions of babies to be exploited; when we declare to the nation; "Show us that the best possible chance in life is given to every child now brought into the world, before you cry for more! At present our children are a glut on the market. You hold infant life cheap. Help us to make the world a fit place for children. When you have done this, we will bear you children,—then we shall be true women." The new morality will express this power and responsibility on the part of women.

"With the realization of the moral responsibility of women," writes Havelock Ellis, "the natural relations of life spring back to their due biological adjustment. Motherhood is restored to its natural sacredness. It becomes the concern of the woman herself, and not of society nor any individual, to determine the conditions under which the child shall be conceived...."

Moreover, woman shall further assert her power by refusing to remain the passive instrument of sensual self-gratification on the part of men. Birth Control, in philosophy and practice, is the destroyer of that dualism of the old sexual code. It denies that the sole purpose of sexual activity is procreation; it also denies that sex should be reduced to the level of sensual lust, or that woman should permit herself to be the instrument of its satisfaction. In increasing and differentiating her love demands, woman must elevate sex into another sphere, whereby it may subserve and enhance the possibility of individual and human expression. Man will gain in this no less than woman; for in the age-old enslavement of woman he has enslaved himself; and in the liberation of womankind, all of humanity will experience the joys of a new and fuller freedom.

On this great fundamental and pivotal point new light has been thrown by Lord Bertrand Dawson, the physician of the King of England. In the remarkable and epoch-making address at the Birmingham Church Congress (referred to in my introduction), he spoke of the supreme morality of the mutual and reciprocal joy in the most intimate relation between man and woman. Without this reciprocity there can be no civilization worthy of the name. Lord Dawson suggested that there should be added to the clauses of marriage in the Prayer Book "the complete realization of the love of this man and this woman one for another," and in support of his contention declared that sex love between husband and wife—apart from parenthood—was something to prize and cherish for its own sake. The Lambeth Conference, he remarked, "envisaged a love invertebrate and joyless," whereas, in his view, natural passion in wedlock was not a thing to be ashamed of or unduly repressed. The pronouncement of the Church of England, as set forth in Resolution 68 of the Lambeth Conference seems to imply condemnation of sex love as such, and to imply sanction of sex love only as a means to an end,—namely, procreation. The Lambeth Resolution stated:

"In opposition to the teaching which under the name of science and religion encourages married people in the deliberate cultivation of sexual union as an end in itself, we steadfastly uphold what must always be regarded as the governing considerations of Christian marriage. One is the primary purpose for which marriage exists—namely, the continuation of the race through the gift and heritage of children; the other is the paramount importance in married life of deliberate and thoughtful self-control."

In answer to this point of view Lord Dawson asserted:

"Sex love has, apart from parenthood, a purport of its own. It is something to prize and to cherish for its own sake. It is an essential part of health and happiness in marriage. And now, if you will allow me, I will carry this argument a step further. If sexual union is a gift of God it is worth learning how to use it. Within its own sphere it should be cultivated so as to bring physical satisfaction to both, not merely to one.... The real problems before us are those of sex love and child love; and by sex love I mean that love which involves intercourse or the desire for such. It is necessary to my argument to emphasize that sex love is one of the dominating forces of the world. Not only does history show the destinies of nations and dynasties determined by its sway—but here in our every-day life we see its influence, direct or indirect, forceful and ubiquitous beyond aught else. Any statesmanlike view, therefore, will recognize that here we have an instinct so fundamental, so imperious, that its influence is a fact which has to be accepted; suppress it you cannot. You may guide it into healthy channels, but an outlet it will have, and if that outlet is inadequate and unduly obstructed irregular channels will be forced....

"The attainment of mutual and reciprocal joy in their relations constitutes a firm bond between two people, and makes for durability of the marriage tie. Reciprocity in sex love is the physical counterpart of sympathy. More marriages fail from inadequate and clumsy sex love than from too much sex love. The lack of proper understanding is in no small measure responsible for the unfulfillment of connubial happiness, and every degree of discontent and unhappiness may, from this cause, occur, leading to rupture of the marriage bond itself. How often do medical men have to deal with these difficulties, and how fortunate if such difficulties are disclosed early enough in married life to be rectified. Otherwise how tragic may be their consequences, and many a case in the Divorce Court has thus had its origin. To the foregoing contentions, it might be objected, you are encouraging passion. My reply would be, passion is a worthy possession—most men, who are any good, are capable of passion. You all enjoy ardent and passionate love in art and literature. Why not give it a place in real life? Why some people look askance at passion is because they are confusing it with sensuality. Sex love without passion is a poor, lifeless thing. Sensuality, on the other hand, is on a level with gluttony—a physical excess—detached from sentiment, chivalry, or tenderness. It is just as important to give sex love its place as to avoid its over-emphasis. Its real and effective restraints are those imposed by a loving and sympathetic companionship, by the privileges of parenthood, the exacting claims of career and that civic sense which prompts men to do social service. Now that the revision of the Prayer Book is receiving consideration, I should like to suggest with great respect an addition made to the objects of marriage in the Marriage Service, in these terms, 'The complete realization of the love of this man and this woman, the one for the other.'"

Turning to the specific problem of Birth Control, Lord Dawson declared, "that Birth Control is here to stay. It is an established fact, and for good or evil has to be accepted. Although the extent of its application can be and is being modified, no denunciations will abolish it. Despite the influence and condemnations of the Church, it has been practised in France for well over half a century, and in Belgium and other Roman Catholic countries is extending. And if the Roman Catholic Church, with its compact organization, its power of authority, and its disciplines, cannot check this procedure, it is not likely that Protestant Churches will be able to do so, for Protestant religions depend for their strength on the conviction and esteem they establish in the heads and hearts of their people. The reasons which lead parents to limit their offspring are sometimes selfish, but more often honorable and cogent."

A report of the Fabian Society[44] on the morality of Birth Control, based upon a census conducted under the chairmanship of Sidney Webb, concludes: "These facts—which we are bound to face whether we like them or not—will appear in different lights to different people. In some quarters it seems to be sufficient to dismiss them with moral indignation, real or simulated. Such a judgment appears both irrelevant and futile.... If a course of conduct is habitually and deliberately pursued by vast multitudes of otherwise well-conducted people, forming probably a majority of the whole educated class of the nation, we must assume that it does not conflict with their actual code of morality. They may be intellectually mistaken, but they are not doing what they feel to be wrong."

The moral justification and ethical necessity of Birth Control need not be empirically based upon the mere approval of experience and custom. Its morality is more profound. Birth Control is an ethical necessity for humanity to-day because it places in our hands a new instrument of self-expression and self-realization. It gives us control over one of the primordial forces of nature, to which in the past the majority of mankind have been enslaved, and by which it has been cheapened and debased. It arouses us to the possibility of newer and greater freedom. It develops the power, the responsibility and intelligence to use this freedom in living a liberated and abundant life. It permits us to enjoy this liberty without danger of infringing upon the similar liberty of our fellow men, or of injuring and curtailing the freedom of the next generation. It shows us that we need not seek in the amassing of worldly wealth, not in the illusion of some extra-terrestrial Heaven or earthly Utopia of a remote future the road to human development. The Kingdom of Heaven is in a very definite sense within us. Not by leaving our body and our fundamental humanity behind us, not by aiming to be anything but what we are, shall we become ennobled or immortal. By knowing ourselves, by expressing ourselves, by realizing ourselves more completely than has ever before been possible, not only shall we attain the kingdom ourselves but we shall hand on the torch of life undimmed to our children and the children of our children.

---

[44] Fabian Tract No. 131.

CHAPTER X: Science the Ally

"There is but one hope. Ignorance, poverty, and vice must stop populating the world. This cannot be done by moral suasion. This cannot be done by talk or example. This cannot be done by religion or by law, by priest or by hangman. This cannot be done by force, physical or moral. To accomplish this there is but one way. Science must make woman the owner, the mistress of herself. Science, the only possible savior of mankind, must put it in the power of woman to decide for herself whether she will or will not become a mother."

Robert G. Ingersoll

"Science is the great instrument of social change," wrote A. J. Balfour in 1908; "all the greater because its object is not change but knowledge, and its silent appropriation of this dominant function, amid the din of religious and political strife, is the most vital of all revolutions which have marked the development of modern civilization." The Birth Control movement has allied itself with science, and no small part of its present propaganda is to awaken the interest of scientists to the pivotal importance to civilization of this instrument. Only with the aid of science is it possible to perfect a practical method that may be universally taught. As Dean Inge recently admitted: "We should be ready to give up all our theories if science proved that we were on the wrong lines."

One of the principal aims of the American Birth Control League has been to awaken the interest of scientific investigators and to point out the rich field for original research opened up by this problem. The correlation of reckless breeding with defective and delinquent strains, has not, strangely enough, been subjected to close scientific scrutiny, nor has the present biological unbalance been traced to its root. This is a crying necessity of our day, and it cannot be accomplished without the aid of science.

Secondary only to the response of women themselves is the awakened interest of scientists, statisticians, and research workers in every field. If the clergy and the defenders of traditional morality have opposed the movement for Birth Control, the response of enlightened scientists and physicians has been one of the most encouraging aids in our battle.

Recent developments in the realm of science,—in psychology, in physiology, in chemistry and physics—all tend to emphasize the immediate necessity for human control over the great forces of nature. The new ideas published by contemporary science are of the utmost fascination and illumination even to the layman. They perform the invaluable task of making us look at life in a new light, of searching close at hand for the solution to heretofore closed mysteries of life. In this brief chapter, I can touch these ideas only as they have proved valuable to me. Professor Soddy's "Science and Life" is one of the most inspiring of recent publications in this field; for this great authority shows us how closely bound up is science with the whole of Society, how science must help to solve the great and disastrous unbalance in human society.

As an example: a whole literature has sprung into being around the glands, the most striking being "The Sex Complex" by Blair Bell. This author advances the idea of the glandular system as an integral whole, the glands forming a unity which might be termed the generative system. Thus is reasserted the radical importance of sexual health to every individual. The whole tendency of modern physiology and psychology, in a word, seems gradually coming to the truth that seemed intuitively to be revealed to that great woman, Olive Schreiner, who, in "Woman and Labor" wrote: "... Noble is the function of physical reproduction of humanity by the union of man and woman. Rightly viewed, that union has in it latent, other and even higher forms of creative energy and life-dispensing power, and... its history on earth has only begun; as the first wild rose when it hung from its stem with its center of stamens and pistils and its single whorl of pale petals had only begun its course, and was destined, as the ages passed, to develop stamen upon stamen and petal upon petal, till it assumed a hundred forms of joy and beauty.

"And it would indeed almost seem, that, on the path toward the higher development of sexual life on earth, as man has so often had to lead in other paths, that here it is perhaps woman, by reason of those very sexual conditions which in the past have crushed and trammeled her, who is bound to lead the way and man to follow. So that it may be at last that sexual love—that tired angel who through the ages has presided over the march of humanity, with distraught eyes, and feather-shafts broken and wings drabbled in the mires of lust and greed, and golden locks caked over with the dust of injustice and oppression—till those looking at him have sometimes cried in terror, `He is the Evil and not the Good of life': and have sought if it were not possible, to exterminate him—shall yet, at last, bathed from the mire and dust of ages in the streams of friendship and freedom, leap upwards, with white wings spread, resplendent in the sunshine of a distant future—the essentially Good and Beautiful of human existence."

To-day science is verifying the truth of this inspiring vision. Certain fundamental truths concerning the basic facts of Nature and humanity especially impress us. A rapid survey may indicate the main features of this mysterious identity and antagonism.

Mankind has gone forward by the capture and control of the forces of Nature. This upward struggle began with the kindling of the first fire. The domestication of animal life marked another great step in the long ascent. The capture of the great physical forces, the discovery of coal and mineral oil, of gas, steam and electricity, and their adaptation to the everyday uses of mankind, wrought the greatest changes in the course of civilization. With the discovery of radium and radioactivity, with the recognition of the vast stores of physical energy concealed in the atom, humanity is now on the eve of a new conquest. But, on the other side, humanity has been compelled to combat continuously those great forces of Nature which have opposed it at every moment of this long indomitable march out of barbarism. Humanity has had to wage war against insects, germs, bacteria, which have spread disease and epidemics and devastation. Humanity has had to adapt itself to those natural forces it could not conquer but could only adroitly turn to its own ends. Nevertheless, all along the line, in colonization, in agriculture, in medicine and in industry, mankind has triumphed over Nature.

But lest the recognition of this victory lead us to self-satisfaction and complacency, we should never forget that this mastery consists to a great extent in a recognition of the power of those blind forces, and our adroit control over them. It has been truly said that we attain no power over Nature until we learn natural laws and conform and adapt ourselves to them.

The strength of the human race has been its ability not merely to subjugate the forces of Nature, but to adapt itself to those it could not conquer. And even this subjugation, science tells us, has not resulted from any attempt to suppress, prohibit, or eradicate these forces, but rather to transform blind and undirected energies to our own purposes.

These great natural forces, science now asserts, are not all external. They are surely concealed within the complex organism of the human being no less than outside of it. These inner forces are no less imperative, no less driving and compelling than the external forces of Nature. As the old conception of the antagonism between body and soul is broken down, as psychology becomes an ally of physiology and biology, and biology joins hands with physics and chemistry, we are taught to see that there is a mysterious unity between these inner and outer forces. They express themselves in accordance with the same structural, physical and chemical laws. The development of civilization in the subjective world, in the sphere of behavior, conduct and morality, has been precisely the gradual accumulation and popularization of methods which teach people how to direct, transform and transmute the driving power of the great natural forces.

Psychology is now recognizing the forces concealed in the human organism. In the long process of adaptation to social life, men have had to harness the wishes and desires born of these inner energies, the greatest and most imperative of which are Sex and Hunger. From the beginning of time, men have been driven by Hunger into a thousand activities. It is Hunger that has created "the struggle for existence." Hunger has spurred men to the discovery and invention of methods and ways of avoiding starvation, of storing and exchanging foods. It has developed primitive barter into our contemporary Wall Streets. It has developed thrift and economy,—expedients whereby humanity avoids the lash of King Hunger. The true "economic interpretation of history" might be termed the History of Hunger.

But no less fundamental, no less imperative, no less ceaseless in its dynamic energy, has been the great force of Sex. We do not yet know the intricate but certainly organic relationship between these two forces. It is obvious that they oppose yet reinforce each other,—driving, lashing, spurring mankind on to new conquests or to certain ruin. Perhaps Hunger and Sex are merely opposite poles of a single great life force. In the past we have made the mistake of separating them and attempting to study one of them without the other. Birth Control emphasizes the need of re-investigation and of knowledge of their integral relationship, and aims at the solution of the great problem of Hunger and Sex at one and the same time.

In the more recent past the effort has been made to control, civilize, and sublimate the great primordial natural force of sex, mainly by futile efforts at prohibition, suppression, restraint, and extirpation. Its revenge, as the psychoanalysts are showing us every day, has been great. Insanity, hysteria, neuroses, morbid fears and compulsions, weaken and render useless and unhappy thousands of humans who are unconscious victims of the attempt to pit individual powers against this great natural force. In the solution of the problem of sex, we should bear in mind what the successful method of humanity has been in its conquest, or rather its control of the great physical and chemical forces of the external world. Like all other energy, that of sex is indestructible. By adaptation, control and conscious direction, we may transmute and sublimate it. Without irreparable injury to ourselves we cannot attempt to eradicate it or extirpate it.

The study of atomic energy, the discovery of radioactivity, and the recognition of potential and latent energies stored in inanimate matter, throw a brilliant illumination upon the whole problem of sex and the inner energies of mankind. Speaking of the discovery of radium, Professor Soddy writes: "Tracked to earth the clew to a great secret for which a thousand telescopes might have swept the sky forever and in vain, lay in a scrap of matter, dowered with something of the same inexhaustible radiance that hitherto has been the sole prerogative of the distant stars and sun." Radium, this distinguished authority tells us, has clothed with its own dignity the whole empire of common matter.

Much as the atomic theory, with its revelations of the vast treasure house of radiant energy that lies all about us, offers new hope in the material world, so the new psychology throws a new light upon human energies and possibilities of individual expression. Social reformers, like those scientists of a bygone era who were sweeping the skies with their telescopes, have likewise been seeking far and wide for the solution of our social problems in remote and wholesale panaceas, whereas the true solution is close at hand,— in the human individual. Buried within each human being lies concealed a vast store of energy, which awaits release, expression and sublimation. The individual may profitably be considered as the "atom" of society. And the solution of the problems of society and of civilization will be brought about when we release the energies now latent and undeveloped in the individual. Professor Edwin Grant Conklin expresses the problem in another form; though his analogy, it seems to me, is open to serious criticism. "The freedom of the individual man," he writes,[45] "is to that of society as the freedom of the single cell is to that of the human being. It is this large freedom of society, rather than the freedom of the individual, which democracy offers to the world, free societies, free states, free nations rather than absolutely free individuals. In all organisms and in all social organizations, the freedom of the minor units must be limited in order that the larger unit may achieve a new and greater freedom, and in social evolution the freedom of individuals must be merged more and more into the larger freedom of society."

This analogy does not bear analysis. Restraint and constraint of individual expression, suppression of individual freedom "for the good of society" has been practised from time immemorial; and its failure is all too evident. There is no antagonism between the good of the individual and the good of society. The moment civilization is wise enough to remove the constraints and prohibitions which now hinder the release of inner energies, most of the larger evils of society will perish of inanition and malnutrition. Remove the moral taboos that now bind the human body and spirit, free the individual from the slavery of tradition, remove the chains of fear from men and women, above all answer their unceasing cries for knowledge that would make possible their self-direction and salvation, and in so doing, you best serve the interests of society at large. Free, rational and self-ruling personality would then take the place of self-made slaves, who are the victims both of external constraints and the playthings of the uncontrolled forces of their own instincts.

Science likewise illuminates the whole problem of genius. Hidden in the common stuff of humanity lies buried this power of self-expression. Modern science is teaching us that genius is not some mysterious gift of the gods, some treasure conferred upon individuals chosen by chance. Nor is it, as Lombroso believed, the result of a pathological and degenerate condition, allied to criminality and madness. Rather is it due to the removal of physiological and psychological inhibitions and constraints which makes possible the release and the channeling of the primordial inner energies of man into full and divine expression. The removal of these inhibitions, so scientists assure us, makes possible more rapid and profound perceptions,—so rapid indeed that they seem to the ordinary human being, practically instantaneous, or intuitive. The qualities of genius are not, therefore, qualities lacking in the common reservoir of humanity, but rather the unimpeded release and direction of powers latent in all of us. This process of course is not necessarily conscious.

This view is substantiated by the opposite problem of feeble-mindedness. Recent researches throw a new light on this problem and the contrasting one

---

[45] Conklin, The Direction of Human Evolution, pp. 125, 126.

of human genius. Mental defect and feeble-mindedness are conceived essentially as retardation, arrest of development, differing in degree so that the victim is either an idiot, an imbecile, feeble-minded or a moron, according to the relative period at which mental development ceases.

Scientific research into the functioning of the ductless glands and their secretions throws a new light on this problem. Not long ago these glands were a complete enigma, owing to the fact that they are not provided with excretory ducts. It has just recently been shown that these organs, such as the thyroid, the pituitary, the suprarenal, the parathyroid and the reproductive glands, exercise an all-powerful influence upon the course of individual development or deficiency. Gley, to whom we owe much of our knowledge of glandular action, has asserted that "the genesis and exercise of the higher faculties of men are conditioned by the purely chemical action of the product of these secretions. Let psychologists consider these facts."

These internal secretions or endocrines pass directly into the blood stream, and exercise a dominating power over health and personality. Deficiency in the thyroid secretion, especially during the years of infancy and early childhood, creates disorders of nutrition and inactivity of the nervous system. The particular form of idiocy known as cretinism is the result of this deficiency, which produces an arrest of the development of the brain cells. The other glands and their secretions likewise exercise the most profound influence upon development, growth and assimilation. Most of these glands are of very small size, none of them larger than a walnut, and some—the parathyroids—almost microscopic. Nevertheless, they are essential to the proper maintenance of life in the body, and no less organically related to mental and psychic development as well.

The reproductive glands, it should not be forgotten, belong to this group, and besides their ordinary products, the germ and sperm cells (ova and spermatozoa) form *hormones* which circulate in the blood and effect changes in the cells of distant parts of the body. Through these *hormones* the secondary sexual characters are produced, including the many differences in the form and structure of the body which are the characteristics of the sexes. Only in recent years has science discovered that these secondary sexual characters are brought about by the agency of these internal secretions or hormones, passed from the reproductive glands into the circulating blood. These so-called secondary characters which are the sign of full and healthy development, are dependent, science tells us, upon the state of development of the reproductive organs.

For a clear and illuminating account of the creative and dynamic power of the endocrine glands, the layman is referred to a recently published book by

Dr. Louis Berman.[46] This authority reveals anew how body and soul are bound up together in a complex unity. Our spiritual and psychic difficulties cannot be solved until we have mastered the knowledge of the wellsprings of our being. "The chemistry of the soul! Magnificent phrase!" exclaims Dr. Berman. "It's a long, long way to that goal. The exact formula is as yet far beyond our reach. But we have started upon the long journey, and we shall get there.

"The internal secretions constitute and determine much of the inherited powers of the individual and their development. They control physical and mental growth, and all the metabolic processes of fundamental importance. They dominate all the vital functions of man during the three cycles of life. They cooperate in an intimate relationship which may be compared to an interlocking directorate. A derangement of their functions, causing an insufficiency of them, an excess, or an abnormality, upsets the entire equilibrium of the body, with transforming effects upon the mind and the organs. In short, they control human nature, and whoever controls them, controls human nature....

"Blood chemistry of our time is a marvel, undreamed of a generation ago. Also, these achievements are a perfect example of the accomplished fact contradicting a prior prediction and criticism. For it was one of the accepted dogmas of the nineteenth century that the phenomena of living could never be subjected to accurate quantitative analysis." But the ethical dogmas of the past, no less than the scientific, may block the way to true civilization.

Physiologically as well as psychologically the development of the human being, the sane mind in the sound body, is absolutely dependent upon the functioning and exercise of all the organs in the body. The "moralists" who preach abstinence, self-denial, and suppression are relegated by these findings of impartial and disinterested science to the class of those educators of the past who taught that it was improper for young ladies to indulge in sports and athletics and who produced generations of feeble, undeveloped invalids, bound up by stays and addicted to swooning and hysterics. One need only go out on the street of any American city to-day to be confronted with the victims of the cruel morality of self-denial and "sin." This fiendish "morality" is stamped upon those emaciated bodies, indelibly written in those emasculated, underdeveloped, undernourished figures of men and women, in the nervous tension and unrelaxed muscles denoting the ceaseless vigilance in restraining and suppressing the expression of natural impulses.

Birth Control is no negative philosophy concerned solely with the number of children brought into this world. It is not merely a question of population. Primarily it is the instrument of liberation and of human development.

---

[46] The Glands Regulating Personality: A study of the glands of internal secretion in relation to the types of human nature. By Louis Berman, M. D., Associate in Biological Chemistry, Columbia University; Physician to the Special Health Clinic. Lenox Hill Hospital. New York: 1921.

It points the way to a morality in which sexual expression and human development will not be in conflict with the interest and well-being of the race nor of contemporary society at large. Not only is it the most effective, in fact the only lever by which the value of the child can be raised to a civilized point; but it is likewise the only method by which the life of the individual can be deepened and strengthened, by which an inner peace and security and beauty may be substituted for the inner conflict that is at present so fatal to self-expression and self-realization.

Sublimation of the sexual instinct cannot take place by denying it expression, nor by reducing it to the plane of the purely physiological. Sexual experience, to be of contributory value, must be integrated and assimilated. Asceticism defeats its own purpose because it develops the obsession of licentious and obscene thoughts, the victim alternating between temporary victory over "sin" and the remorse of defeat. But the seeker of purely physical pleasure, the libertine or the average sensualist, is no less a pathological case, living as one-sided and unbalanced a life as the ascetic, for his conduct is likewise based on ignorance and lack of understanding. In seeking pleasure without the exercise of responsibility, in trying to get something for nothing, he is not merely cheating others but himself as well.

In still another field science and scientific method now emphasize the pivotal importance of Birth Control. The Binet-Simon intelligence tests which have been developed, expanded, and applied to large groups of children and adults present positive statistical data concerning the mental equipment of the type of children brought into the world under the influence of indiscriminate fecundity and of those fortunate children who have been brought into the world because they are wanted, the children of conscious, voluntary procreation, well nourished, properly clothed, the recipients of all that proper care and love can accomplish.

In considering the data furnished by these intelligence tests we should remember several factors that should be taken into consideration. Irrespective of other considerations, children who are underfed, undernourished, crowded into badly ventilated and unsanitary homes and chronically hungry cannot be expected to attain the mental development of children upon whom every advantage of intelligent and scientific care is bestowed. Furthermore, public school methods of dealing with children, the course of studies prescribed, may quite completely fail to awaken and develop the intelligence.

The statistics indicate at any rate a surprisingly low rate of intelligence among the classes in which large families and uncontrolled procreation predominate. Those of the lowest grade in intelligence are born of unskilled laborers (with the highest birth rate in the community); the next high among the skilled laborers, and so on to the families of professional people, among whom it is now admitted that the birth rate is voluntarily controlled.[47]

But scientific investigations of this type cannot be complete until statistics are accurately obtained concerning the relation of unrestrained fecundity and the quality, mental and physical, of the children produced. The philosophy of Birth Control therefore seeks and asks the cooperation of science and scientists, not to strengthen its own "case," but because this sexual factor in the determination of human history has so long been ignored by historians and scientists. If science in recent years has contributed enormously to strengthen the conviction of all intelligent people of the necessity and wisdom of Birth Control, this philosophy in its turn opens to science in its various fields a suggestive avenue of approach to many of those problems of humanity and society which at present seem to enigmatical and insoluble.

---

[47] Cf Terman: Intelligence of School Children. New York 1919. p. 56. Also, "Is America Safe for Democracy?" Six lectures given at the Lowell Institute of Boston, by William McDougall, Professor of Psychology in Harvard College. New York, 1921.

CHAPTER XI: Education and Expression

"Civilization is bound up with the success of that movement. The man who rejoices in it and strives to further it is alive; the man who shudders and raises impotent hands against it is merely dead, even though the grave yet yawns for him in vain. He may make dead laws and preach dead sermons and his sermons may be great and his laws may be rigid. But as the wisest of men saw twenty-five centuries ago, the things that are great and strong and rigid are the things that stay below in the grave. It is the things that are delicate and tender and supple that stay above. At no point is life so tender and delicate and supple as at the point of sex. There is the triumph of life."

Havelock Ellis

Our approach opens to us a fresh scale of values, a new and effective method of testing the merits and demerits of current policies and programs. It redirects our attention to the great source and fountainhead of human life. It offers us the most strategic point of view from which to observe and study the unending drama of humanity,—how the past, the present and the future of the human race are all organically bound up together. It coordinates heredity and environment. Most important of all, it frees the mind of sexual prejudice and taboo, by demanding the frankest and most unflinching reexamination of sex in its relation to human nature and the bases of human society. In aiding to establish this mental liberation, quite apart from any of the tangible results that might please the statistically-minded, the study of Birth Control is performing an invaluable task. Without complete mental freedom, it is impossible to approach any fundamental human problem. Failure to face the great central facts of sex in an impartial and scientific spirit lies at the root of the blind opposition to Birth Control.

Our bitterest opponents must agree that the problem of Birth Control is one of the most important that humanity to-day has to face. The interests of the entire world, of humanity, of the future of mankind itself are more at stake in this than wars, political institutions, or industrial reorganization. All other projects of reform, of revolution or reconstruction, are of secondary importance, even trivial, when we compare them to the wholesale regeneration—or disintegration—that is bound up with the control, the direction and the release of one of the greatest forces in nature. The great danger at present does not lie with the bitter opponents of the idea of Birth Control, nor with those who are attempting to suppress our program of enlightenment and education. Such opposition is always stimulating. It wins new adherents. It reveals its own weakness and lack of insight. The greater danger is to be found in the flaccid, undiscriminating interest of "sympathizers" who are "for it"—as an accessory to their own particular panacea. "It even seems, sometimes," wrote the late William Graham Sumner, "as if the primitive people were working along better lines of effort in this direction than we are... when our public organs of instruction taboo all that pertains to reproduction as improper; and when public authority, ready enough to interfere with personal liberty everywhere else, feels bound to act as if there were no societal interest at stake in the begetting of the next generation."[48]

Slowly but surely we are breaking down the taboos that surround sex; but we are breaking them down out of sheer necessity. The codes that have surrounded sexual behavior in the so-called Christian communities, the teachings of the churches concerning chastity and sexual purity, the prohibitions of the laws, and the hypocritical conventions of society, have all demonstrated their failure as safeguards against the chaos produced and the havoc wrought by the failure to recognize sex as a driving force in human nature,—as great as, if indeed not greater than, hunger. Its dynamic energy is indestructible. It may be transmuted, refined, directed, even sublimated, but to ignore, to neglect, to refuse to recognize this great elemental force is nothing less than foolhardy.

Out of the unchallenged policies of continence, abstinence, "chastity" and "purity," we have reaped the harvests of prostitution, venereal scourges and innumerable other evils. Traditional moralists have failed to recognize that chastity and purity must be the outward symptoms of awakened intelligence, of satisfied desires, and fulfilled love. They cannot be taught by "sex education." They cannot be imposed from without by a denial of the might and the right of sexual expression. Nevertheless, even in the contemporary teaching of sex hygiene and social prophylaxis, nothing constructive is offered to young men and young women who seek aid through the trying period of adolescence.

At the Lambeth Conference of 1920, the Bishops of the Church of England stated in their report on their considerations of sexual morality: "Men should regard all women as they do their mothers, sisters, and daughters; and women should dress only in such a manner as to command respect from every man. All right-minded persons should unite in the suppression of pernicious literature, plays and films...." Could lack of psychological insight and understanding be more completely indicated? Yet, like these bishops, most of those who are undertaking the education of the young are as ignorant themselves of psychology and physiology. Indeed, those who are speaking belatedly of the need of "sexual hygiene" seem to be unaware that they themselves are most in need of it. "We must give up the futile attempt to keep young people in the dark," cries Rev. James Marchant in "Birth-Rate and Empire," "and the assumption that they are ignorant of notorious facts. We

---

[48] Folkways, p. 492.

cannot, if we would, stop the spread of sexual knowledge; and if we could do so, we would only make matters infinitely worse. This is the second decade of the twentieth century, not the early Victorian period.... It is no longer a question of knowing or not knowing. We have to disabuse our middle-aged minds of that fond delusion. Our young people know more than we did when we began our married lives, and sometimes as much as we know, ourselves, even now. So that we need not continue to shake our few remaining hairs in simulating feelings of surprise or horror. It might have been better for us if we had been more enlightened. And if our discussion of this problem is to be of any real use, we must at the outset reconcile ourselves to the fact that the birth-rate is voluntarily controlled.... Certain persons who instruct us in these matters hold up their pious hands and whiten their frightened faces as they cry out in the public squares against 'this vice,' but they can only make themselves ridiculous."

Taught upon the basis of conventional and traditional morality and middle-class respectability, based on current dogma, and handed down to the populace with benign condescension, sex education is a waste of time and effort. Such education cannot in any true sense set up as a standard the ideal morality and behavior of the respectable middle-class and then make the effort to induce all other members of society, especially the working classes, to conform to their taboos. Such a method is not only confusing, but, in the creation of strain and hysteria and an unhealthy concentration upon moral conduct, results in positive injury. To preach a negative and colorless ideal of chastity to young men and women is to neglect the primary duty of awakening their intelligence, their responsibility, their self-reliance and independence. Once this is accomplished, the matter of chastity will take care of itself. The teaching of "etiquette" must be superseded by the teaching of hygiene. Hygienic habits are built up upon a sound knowledge of bodily needs and functions. It is only in the sphere of sex that there remains an unfounded fear of presenting without the gratuitous introduction of non-essential taboos and prejudice, unbiased and unvarnished facts.

As an instrument of education, the doctrine of Birth Control approaches the whole problem in another manner. Instead of laying down hard and fast laws of sexual conduct, instead of attempting to inculcate rules and regulations, of pointing out the rewards of virtue and the penalties of "sin" (as is usually attempted in relation to the venereal diseases), the teacher of Birth Control seeks to meet the needs of the people. Upon the basis of their interests, their demands, their problems, Birth Control education attempts to develop their intelligence and show them how they may help themselves; how to guide and control this deep-rooted instinct.

The objection has been raised that Birth Control only reaches the already enlightened, the men and women who have already attained a degree of self-respect and self-reliance. Such an objection could not be based on fact. Even in the most unenlightened sections of the community, among mothers crushed by poverty and economic enslavement, there is the realization of the evils of the too-large family, of the rapid succession of pregnancy after pregnancy, of the hopelessness of bringing too many children into the world. Not merely in the evidence presented in an earlier chapter but in other ways, is this crying need expressed. The investigators of the Children's Bureau who collected the data of the infant mortality reports, noted the willingness and the eagerness with which these down-trodden mothers told the truth about themselves. So great is their hope of relief from that meaningless and deadening submission to unproductive reproduction, that only a society pruriently devoted to hypocrisy could refuse to listen to the voices of these mothers. Respectfully we lend our ears to dithyrambs about the sacredness of motherhood and the value of "better babies"—but we shut our eyes and our ears to the unpleasant reality and the cries of pain that come from women who are to-day dying by the thousands because this power is withheld from them.

This situation is rendered more bitterly ironic because the self-righteous opponents of Birth Control practise themselves the doctrine they condemn. The birth-rate among conservative opponents indicates that they restrict the numbers of their own children by the methods of Birth Control, or are of such feeble procreative energy as to be thereby unfitted to dictate moral laws for other people. They prefer that we should think their small number of children is accidental, rather than publicly admit the successful practice of intelligent foresight. Or else they hold themselves up as paragons of virtue and self-control, and would have us believe that they have brought their children into the world solely from a high, stern sense of public duty—an attitude which is about as convincing as it would be to declare that they found them under gooseberry bushes. How else can we explain the widespread tolerance and smug approval of the clerical idea of sex, now re-enforced by floods of crude and vulgar sentiment, which is promulgated by the press, motion-pictures and popular plays?

Like all other education, that of sex can be rendered effective and valuable only as it meets and satisfies the interests and demands of the pupil himself. It cannot be imposed from without, handed down from above, superimposed upon the intelligence of the person taught. It must find a response within him, give him the power and the instrument wherewith he may exercise his own growing intelligence, bring into action his own judgment and discrimination and thus contribute to the growth of his intelligence. The civilized world is coming to see that education cannot consist merely in the assimilation of external information and knowledge, but rather in the awakening and development of innate powers of discrimination and judgment. The great disaster of "sex education" lies in the fact that it fails to direct the awakened interests of the pupils into the proper channels of exercise and development. Instead, it blunts them, restricts them, hinders them, and even attempts to eradicate them.

This has been the great defect of sex education as it has been practised in recent years. Based on a superficial and shameful view of the sexual instinct, it has sought the inculcation of negative virtues by pointing out the sinister penalties of promiscuity, and by advocating strict adherence to virtue and morality, not on the basis of intelligence or the outcome of experience, not even for the attainment of rewards, but merely to avoid punishment in the form of painful and malignant disease. Education so conceived carries with it its own refutation. True education cannot tolerate the inculcation of fear. Fear is the soil in which are implanted inhibitions and morbid compulsions. Fear restrains, restricts, hinders human expression. It strikes at the very roots of joy and happiness. It should therefore be the aim of sex education to avoid above all the implanting of fear in the mind of the pupil.

Restriction means placing in the hands of external authority the power over behavior. Birth Control, on the contrary, implies voluntary action, the decision for one's self how many children one shall or shall not bring into the world. Birth Control is educational in the real sense of the word, in that it asserts this power of decision, reinstates this power in the people themselves.

We are not seeking to introduce new restrictions but greater freedom. As far as sex is concerned, the impulse has been more thoroughly subject to restriction than any other human instinct. "Thou shalt not!" meets us at every turn. Some of these restrictions are justified; some of them are not. We may have but one wife or one husband at a time; we must attain a certain age before we may marry. Children born out of wedlock are deemed "illegitimate"—even healthy children. The newspapers every day are filled with the scandals of those who have leaped over the restrictions or limitations society has written in her sexual code. Yet the voluntary control of the procreative powers, the rational regulation of the number of children we bring into the world—this is the one type of restriction frowned upon and prohibited by law!

In a more definite, a much more realistic and concrete manner, Birth Control reveals itself as the most effective weapon in the spread of hygienic and prophylactic knowledge among women of the less fortunate classes. It carries with it a thorough training in bodily cleanliness and physiology, a definite knowledge of the physiology and function of sex. In refusing to teach both sides of the subject, in failing to respond to the universal demand among women for such instruction and information, maternity centers limit their own efforts and fail to fulfil what should be their true mission. They are concerned merely with pregnancy, maternity, child-bearing, the problem of keeping the baby alive. But any effective work in this field must go further back. We have gradually come to see, as Havelock Ellis has pointed out, that comparatively little can be done by improving merely the living conditions of adults; that improving conditions for children and babies is not enough. To combat the evils of infant mortality, natal and pre-natal care is not sufficient. Even to improve the conditions for the pregnant woman, is insufficient. Necessarily and inevitably, we are led further and further back, to the point of procreation; beyond that, into the regulation of sexual selection. The problem becomes a circle. We cannot solve one part of it without a consideration of the entirety. But it is especially at the point of creation where all the various forces are concentrated. Conception must be controlled by reason, by intelligence, by science, or we lose control of all its consequences.

Birth Control is essentially an education for women. It is women who, directly and by their very nature, bear the burden of that blindness, ignorance and lack of foresight concerning sex which is now enforced by law and custom. Birth Control places in the hands of women the only effective instrument whereby they may reestablish the balance in society, and assert, not only theoretically but practically as well, the primary importance of the woman and the child in civilization.

Birth Control is thus the stimulus to education. Its exercise awakens and develops the sense of self-reliance and responsibility, and illuminates the relation of the individual to society and to the race in a manner that otherwise remains vague and academic. It reveals sex not merely as an untamed and insatiable natural force to which men and women must submit hopelessly and inertly, as it sweeps through them, and then accept with abject humility the hopeless and heavy consequences. Instead, it places in their hands the power to control this great force; to use it, to direct it into channels in which it becomes the energy enhancing their lives and increasing self-expression and self-development. It awakens in women the consciousness of new glories and new possibilities in motherhood. No longer the prostrate victim of the blind play of instinct but the self-reliant mistress of her body and her own will, the new mother finds in her child the fulfilment of her own desires. In free instead of compulsory motherhood she finds the avenue of her own development and expression. No longer bound by an unending series of pregnancies, at liberty to safeguard the development of her own children, she may now extend her beneficent influence beyond her own home. In becoming thus intensified, motherhood may also broaden and become more extensive as well. The mother sees that the welfare of her own children is bound up with the welfare of all others. Not upon the basis of sentimental charity or gratuitous "welfare-work" but upon that of enlightened self-interest, such a mother may exert her influence among the less fortunate and less enlightened.

Unless based upon this central knowledge of and power over her own body and her own instincts, education for woman is valueless. As long as she remains the plaything of strong, uncontrolled natural forces, as long as she must docilely and humbly submit to the decisions of others, how can woman ever lay the foundations of self-respect, self-reliance and independence? How can she make her own choice, exercise her own discrimination, her own foresight?

In the exercise of these powers, in the building up and integration of her own experience, in mastering her own environment the true education of woman must be sought. And in the sphere of sex, the great source and root of all human experience, it is upon the basis of Birth Control—the voluntary direction of her own sexual expression—that woman must take her first step in the assertion of freedom and self-respect.

CHAPTER XII: Woman and the Future

*I saw a woman sleeping. In her sleep she dreamed Life stood
before her, and held in each hand a gift—in the one Love, in the
other Freedom. And she said to the woman, "Choose!"*

And the woman waited long: and she said, "Freedom!"

*And Life said, "Thou has well chosen. If thou hadst said, `Love,'
I would have given thee that thou didst ask for; and I would have
gone from thee, and returned to thee no more. Now, the day will
come when I shall return. In that day I shall bear both gifts in one
hand."*

I heard the woman laugh in her sleep.

Olive Schreiner

By no means is it necessary to look forward to some vague and distant date
of the future to test the benefits which the human race derives from the
program I have suggested in the preceding pages. The results to the individual
woman, to the family, and to the State, particularly in the case of Holland,
have already been investigated and recorded. Our philosophy is no doctrine of
escape from the immediate and pressing realities of life, on the contrary, we
say to men and women, and particularly to the latter: face the realities of your
own soul and body; know thyself! And in this last admonition, we mean that
this knowledge should not consist of some vague shopworn generalities about
the nature of woman—woman as created in the minds of men, nor woman
putting herself on a romantic pedestal above the harsh facts of this workaday
world. Women can attain freedom only by concrete, definite knowledge of
themselves, a knowledge based on biology, physiology and psychology.

Nevertheless it would be wrong to shut our eyes to the vision of a world of
free men and women, a world which would more closely resemble a garden
than the present jungle of chaotic conflicts and fears. One of the greatest
dangers of social idealists, to all of us who hope to make a better world, is to
seek refuge in highly colored fantasies of the future rather than to face and
combat the bitter and evil realities which to-day on all sides confront us. I
believe that the reader of my preceding chapters will not accuse me of
shirking these realities; indeed, he may think that I have overemphasized the
great biological problems of defect, delinquency and bad breeding. It is in the
hope that others too may glimpse my vision of a world regenerated that I
submit the following suggestions. They are based on the belief that we must
seek individual and racial health not by great political or social reconstruction,
but, turning to a recognition of our own inherent powers and development, by

the release of our inner energies. It is thus that all of us can best aid in making of this world, instead of a vale of tears, a garden.

Let us first of all consider merely from the viewpoint of business and "efficiency" the biological or racial problems which confront us. As Americans, we have of late made much of "efficiency" and business organization. Yet would any corporation for one moment conduct its affairs as we conduct the infinitely more important affairs of our civilization? Would any modern stockbreeder permit the deterioration of his livestock as we not only permit but positively encourage the destruction and deterioration of the most precious, the most essential elements in our world community—the mothers and children. With the mothers and children thus cheapened, the next generation of men and women is inevitably below par. The tendency of the human elements, under present conditions, is constantly downward.

Turn to Robert M. Yerkes's "Psychological Examining in the United States Army"[49] in which we are informed that the psychological examination of the drafted men indicated that nearly half—47.3 per cent.—of the population had the mentality of twelve-year-old children or less—in other words that they are morons. Professor Conklin, in his recently published volume "The Direction of Human Evolution"[50] is led, on the findings of Mr. Yerkes's report, to assert: "Assuming that these drafted men are a fair sample of the entire population of approximately 100,000,000, this means that 45,000,000 or nearly one-half the entire population, will never develop mental capacity beyond the stage represented by a normal twelve-year-old child, and that only 13,500,000 will ever show superior intelligence."

Making all due allowances for the errors and discrepancies of the psychological examination, we are nevertheless face to face with a serious and destructive practice. Our "overhead" expense in segregating the delinquent, the defective and the dependent, in prisons, asylums and permanent homes, our failure to segregate morons who are increasing and multiplying—I have sufficiently indicated, though in truth I have merely scratched the surface of this international menace—demonstrate our foolhardy and extravagant sentimentalism. No industrial corporation could maintain its existence upon such a foundation. Yet hardheaded "captains of industry," financiers who pride themselves upon their cool-headed and keen-sighted business ability are dropping millions into rosewater philanthropies and charities that are silly at best and vicious at worst. In our dealings with such elements there is a bland maladministration and misuse of huge sums that

---

[49] Memoirs of the National Academy of Sciences. Volume XV.

[50] Conklin, The Direction of Human Evolution. "When it is remembered that mental capacity is inherited, that parents of low intelligence generally produce children of low intelligence, and that on the average they have more children than persons of high intelligence, and furthermore, when we consider that the intellectual capacity or 'mental age' can be changed very little by education, we are in a position to appreciate the very serious condition which confronts us as a nation." p. 108.

should in all righteousness be used for the development and education of the healthy elements of the community.

At the present time, civilized nations are penalizing talent and genius, the bearers of the torch of civilization, to coddle and perpetuate the choking human undergrowth, which, as all authorities tell us, is escaping control and threatens to overrun the whole garden of humanity. Yet men continue to drug themselves with the opiate of optimism, or sink back upon the cushions of Christian resignation, their intellectual powers anaesthetized by cheerful platitudes. Or else, even those, who are fully cognizant of the chaos and conflict, seek an escape in those pretentious but fundamentally fallacious social philosophies which place the blame for contemporary world misery upon anybody or anything except the indomitable but uncontrolled instincts of living organisms. These men fight with shadows and forget the realities of existence. Too many centuries have we sought to hide from the inevitable, which confronts us at every step throughout life.

Let us conceive for the moment at least, a world not burdened by the weight of dependent and delinquent classes, a total population of mature, intelligent, critical and expressive men and women. Instead of the inert, exploitable, mentally passive class which now forms the barren substratum of our civilization, try to imagine a population active, resistant, passing individual and social lives of the most contented and healthy sort. Would such men and women, liberated from our endless, unceasing struggle against mass prejudice and inertia, be deprived in any way of the stimulating zest of life? Would they sink into a slough of complacency and fatuity?

No! Life for them would be enriched, intensified and ennobled in a fashion it is difficult for us in our spiritual and physical squalor even to imagine. There would be a new renaissance of the arts and sciences. Awakened at last to the proximity of the treasures of life lying all about them, the children of that age would be inspired by a spirit of adventure and romance that would indeed produce a terrestrial paradise.

Let us look forward to this great release of creative and constructive energy, not as an idle, vacuous mirage, but as a promise which we, as the whole human race, have it in our power, in the very conduct of our lives from day to day, to transmute into a glorious reality. Let us look forward to that era, perhaps not so distant as we believe, when the great adventures in the enchanted realm of the arts and sciences may no longer be the privilege of a gifted few, but the rightful heritage of a race of genius. In such a world men and women would no longer seek escape from themselves by the fantastic and the faraway. They would be awakened to the realization that the source of life, of happiness, is to be found not outside themselves, but within, in the healthful exercise of their God-given functions. The treasures of life are not hidden; they are close at hand, so close that we overlook them. We cheat ourselves with a pitiful fear of ourselves. Men and women of the future will not seek happiness; they will have gone beyond it. Mere happiness would produce monotony. And their lives shall be lives of change and variety with the thrills produced by experiment and research.

Fear will have been abolished: first of all, the fear of outside things and other people; finally the fear of oneself. And with these fears must disappear forever all those poisons of hatreds, individual and international. For the realization would come that there would be no reason for, no value in encroaching upon, the freedom of one another. To-day we are living in a world which is like a forest of trees too thickly planted. Hence the ferocious, unending struggle for existence. Like innumerable ages past, the present age is one of mutual destruction. Our aim is to substitute cooperation, equity, and amity for antagonism and conflict. If the aim of our country or our civilization is to attain a hollow, meaningless superiority over others in aggregate wealth and population, it may be sound policy to shut our eyes to the sacrifice of human life,—unregarded life and suffering—and to stimulate rapid procreation. But even so, such a policy is bound in the long run to defeat itself, as the decline and fall of great civilizations of the past emphatically indicate. Even the bitterest opponent of our ideals would refuse to subscribe to a philosophy of mere quantity, of wealth and population lacking in spiritual direction or significance. All of us hope for and look forward to the fine flowering of human genius—of genius not expending and dissipating its energy in the bitter struggle for mere existence, but developing to a fine maturity, sustained and nourished by the soil of active appreciation, criticism, and recognition.

Not by denying the central and basic biological facts of our nature, not by subscribing to the glittering but false values of any philosophy or program of escape, not by wild Utopian dreams of the brotherhood of men, not by any sanctimonious debauch of sentimentality or religiosity, may we accomplish the first feeble step toward liberation. On the contrary, only by firmly planting our feet on the solid ground of scientific fact may we even stand erect—may we even rise from the servile stooping posture of the slave, borne down by the weight of age-old oppression.

In looking forward to this radiant release of the inner energies of a regenerated humanity, I am not thinking merely of inventions and discoveries and the application of these to the perfecting of the external and mechanical details of social life. This external and scientific perfecting of the mechanism of external life is a phenomenon we are to a great extent witnessing today. But in a deeper sense this tendency can be of no true or lasting value if it cannot be made to subserve the biological and spiritual development of the human organism, individual and collective. Our great problem is not merely to perfect machinery, to produce superb ships, motor cars or great buildings, but to remodel the race so that it may equal the amazing progress we see now making in the externals of life. We must first free our bodies from disease and predisposition to disease. We must perfect these bodies and make them fine instruments of the mind and the spirit. Only thus, when the body becomes an aid instead of a hindrance to human expression may we attain any civilization worthy of the name. Only thus may we create our bodies a fitting temple for the soul, which is nothing but a vague unreality except insofar as it is able to manifest itself in the beauty of the concrete.

Once we have accomplished the first tentative steps toward the creation of a real civilization, the task of freeing the spirit of mankind from the bondage of ignorance, prejudice and mental passivity which is more fettering now than ever in the history of humanity, will be facilitated a thousand-fold. The great central problem, and one which must be taken first is the abolition of the shame and fear of sex. We must teach men the overwhelming power of this radiant force. We must make them understand that uncontrolled, it is a cruel tyrant, but that controlled and directed, it may be used to transmute and sublimate the everyday world into a realm of beauty and joy. Through sex, mankind may attain the great spiritual illumination which will transform the world, which will light up the only path to an earthly paradise. So must we necessarily and inevitably conceive of sex-expression. The instinct is here. None of us can avoid it. It is in our power to make it a thing of beauty and a joy forever: or to deny it, as have the ascetics of the past, to revile this expression and then to pay the penalty, the bitter penalty that Society to-day is paying in innumerable ways.

If I am criticized for the seeming "selfishness" of this conception it will be through a misunderstanding. The individual is fulfiling his duty to society as a whole by not self-sacrifice but by self-development. He does his best for the world not by dying for it, not by increasing the sum total of misery, disease and unhappiness, but by increasing his own stature, by releasing a greater energy, by being active instead of passive, creative instead of destructive. This is fundamentally the greatest truth to be discovered by womankind at large. And until women are awakened to their pivotal function in the creation of a new civilization, that new era will remain an impossible and fantastic dream. The new civilization can become a glorious reality only with the awakening of woman's now dormant qualities of strength, courage, and vigor. As a great thinker of the last century pointed out, not only to her own health and happiness is the physical degeneracy of woman destructive, but to our whole race. The physical and psychic power of woman is more indispensable to the well-being and power of the human race than that even of man, for the strength and happiness of the child is more organically united with that of the mother.

Parallel with the awakening of woman's interest in her own fundamental nature, in her realization that her greatest duty to society lies in self-realization, will come a greater and deeper love for all of humanity. For in attaining a true individuality of her own she will understand that we are all individuals, that each human being is essentially implicated in every question or problem which involves the well-being of the humblest of us. So to-day we are not to meet the great problems of defect and delinquency in any merely sentimental or superficial manner, but with the firmest and most unflinching attitude toward the true interest of our fellow beings. It is from no mere feeling of brotherly love or sentimental philanthropy that we women must insist upon enhancing the value of child life. It is because we know that, if our children are to develop to their full capabilities, all children must be assured a similar opportunity. Every single case of inherited defect, every malformed child, every congenitally tainted human being brought into this world is of infinite importance to that poor individual; but it is of scarcely less importance to the rest of us and to all of our children who must pay in one way or another for these biological and racial mistakes. We look forward in our vision of the future to children brought into the world because they are desired, called from the unknown by a fearless and conscious passion, because women and men need children to complete the symmetry of their own development, no less than to perpetuate the race. They shall be called into a world enhanced and made beautiful by the spirit of freedom and romance—into a world wherein the creatures of our new day, unhampered and unbound by the sinister forces of prejudice and immovable habit, may work out their own destinies. Perhaps we may catch fragmentary glimpses of this new life in certain societies of the past, in Greece perhaps; but in all of these past civilizations these happy groups formed but a small exclusive section of the population. To-day our task is greater; for we realize that no section of humanity can be reclaimed without the regeneration of the whole.

I look, therefore, into a Future when men and women will not dissipate their energy in the vain and fruitless search for content outside of themselves, in far-away places or people. Perfect masters of their own inherent powers, controlled with a fine understanding of the art of life and of love, adapting themselves with pliancy and intelligence to the milieu in which they find themselves, they will unafraid enjoy life to the utmost. Women will for the first time in the unhappy history of this globe establish a true equilibrium and "balance of power" in the relation of the sexes. The old antagonism will have disappeared, the old ill-concealed warfare between men and women. For the men themselves will comprehend that in this cultivation of the human garden they will be rewarded a thousand times. Interest in the vague sentimental fantasies of extra-mundane existence, in pathological or hysterical flights from the realities of our earthliness, will have through atrophy disappeared, for in that dawn men and women will have come to the realization, already suggested, that here close at hand is our paradise, our everlasting abode, our Heaven and our eternity. Not by leaving it and our essential humanity behind us, nor by sighing to be anything but what we are, shall we ever become ennobled or immortal. Not for woman only, but for all of humanity is this the field where we must seek the secret of eternal life.

APPENDIX

PRINCIPLES AND AIMS OF THE AMERICAN BIRTH CONTROL LEAGUE

PRINCIPLES:

The complex problems now confronting America as the result of the practice of reckless procreation are fast threatening to grow beyond human control.

Everywhere we see poverty and large families going hand in hand. Those least fit to carry on the race are increasing most rapidly. People who cannot support their own offspring are encouraged by Church and State to produce large families. Many of the children thus begotten are diseased or feeble-minded; many become criminals. The burden of supporting these unwanted types has to be bourne by the healthy elements of the nation. Funds that should be used to raise the standard of our civilization are diverted to the maintenance of those who should never have been born.

In addition to this grave evil we witness the appalling waste of women's health and women's lives by too frequent pregnancies. These unwanted pregnancies often provoke the crime of abortion, or alternatively multiply the number of child-workers and lower the standard of living.

To create a race of well born children it is essential that the function of motherhood should be elevated to a position of dignity, and this is impossible as long as conception remains a matter of chance.

We hold that children should be

1. Conceived in love;

2. Born of the mother's conscious desire;

3. And only begotten under conditions which render possible the heritage of health.

Therefore we hold that every woman must possess the power and freedom to prevent conception except when these conditions can be satisfied.

Every mother must realize her basic position in human society. She must be conscious of her responsibility to the race in bringing children into the world.

Instead of being a blind and haphazard consequence of uncontrolled instinct, motherhood must be made the responsible and self-directed means of human expression and regeneration.

These purposes, which are of fundamental importance to the whole of our nation and to the future of mankind, can only be attained if women first receive practical scientific education in the means of Birth Control. That, therefore, is the first object to which the efforts of this League will be directed.

AIMS:

The American Birth Control League aims to enlighten and educate all sections of the American public in the various aspects of the dangers of uncontrolled procreation and the imperative necessity of a world program of Birth Control.

The League aims to correlate the findings of scientists, statisticians, investigators, and social agencies in all fields. To make this possible, it is necessary to organize various departments:

RESEARCH: To collect the findings of scientists, concerning the relation of reckless breeding to the evils of delinquency, defect and dependence.

INVESTIGATION: To derive from these scientifically ascertained facts and figures, conclusions which may aid all public health and social agencies in the study of problems of maternal and infant mortality, child-labor, mental and physical defects and delinquence in relation to the practice of reckless parentage.

HYGIENIC AND PHYSIOLOGICAL instruction by the Medical pro-fession to mothers and potential mothers in harmless and reliable methods of Birth Control in answer to their requests for such knowledge.

STERILIZATION of the insane and feebleminded and the encouragement of this operation upon those afflicted with inherited or transmissible diseases, with the understanding that sterilization does not deprive the individual of his or her sex expression, but merely renders him incapable of producing children.

EDUCATIONAL: The program of education includes: The enlightenment of the public at large, mainly through the education of leaders of thought and opinion—teachers, ministers, editors and writers—to the moral and scientific soundness of the principles of Birth Control and the imperative necessity of its adoption as the basis of national and racial progress.

POLITICAL AND LEGISLATIVE: To enlist the support and cooperation of legal advisers, statesmen and legislators in effecting the removal of state and federal statutes which encourage dysgenic breeding, increase the sum total of disease, misery and poverty and prevent the establishment of a policy of national health and strength.

ORGANIZATION: To send into the various States of the Union field workers to enlist the support and arouse the interest of the masses, to the importance of Birth Control so that laws may be changed and the establishment of clinics made possible in every State.

INTERNATIONAL: This department aims to cooperate with similar organizations in other countries to study Birth Control in its relations to the world population problem, food supplies, national and racial conflicts, and to urge upon all international bodies organized to promote world peace, the consideration of these aspects of international amity.

THE AMERICAN BIRTH CONTROL LEAGUE proposes to publish in its official organ "The Birth Control Review," reports and studies on the relationship of controlled and uncontrolled populations to national and world problems.

The American Birth Control League also proposes to hold an annual Conference to bring together the workers of the various departments so that each worker may realize the inter-relationship of all the various phases of the problem to the end that National education will tend to encourage and develop the powers of self-direction, self-reliance, and independence in the individuals of the community instead of dependence for relief upon public or private charities.

Index